The Little Book of Bathroom Philosophy

THE LITTLE BOOK OF

# Bathroom Philosophy

daily wisdom from the world's greatest thinkers

GREGORY BERGMAN

GLOUCESTER, MASSACHUSETTS

First published in the USA in 2004 by
Fair Winds Press
33 Commercial Street
Gloucester, MA 01930



**Library of Congress Cataloging-in-Publication Data available**

ISBN 1-59233-075-4

2003022329

10 9 8 7 6 5 4 3 2 1

Cover illustration by James Carson

Printed and bound in Canada

To my Mother, whose help, love, and insight
are beyond measure.

# contents

# introduction

## The What and Why of Philosophy

So what is philosophy, anyway? Philosophy is not just an outlook on life, as the word is commonly used. When a drunk sits down next to you at a bar and says, "My philosophy of life is . . . " that is not a philosophy. (Unless, of course, the drunk is an accomplished philosopher who happens to be out for a nightcap.) No, philosophy is a specific discipline.

Before biology and physics were called "sciences" and the study of the mind was called "psychology," and the study of politics was designated "political science," all of these distinct disciplines were practiced and, in a sense, invented by, philosophers. But more than the practice of these disciplines, philosophy is the attempt to develop a comprehensive view of the universe at its most fundamental, as well as a comprehensive view of human beings, from their essential nature to the power and limits of their capabilities.

Philosophy developed out of the desire to uncover the nature of things. It arose as a specific method of understanding the mysteries of the world. The philosophical method advocates the use of logical argument to determine the truth of a claim about the universe.

Philosophers had a desire to uncover the nature of things and created philosophy as a specific method of understanding the mysteries of the world, which gave them a means by which to prove their views. Philosophy differs from religion because its claims about the world are justified by logic, whereas religion explains its principles by way of anecdotes and storytelling.

Even the great novelists, whose ideas about human beings and the world jump off the page, dazzling us with their depth and insight, are not philosophers. Why not? Simply because they are not doing philosophy. That is to say, they offer no explanation or proof of their claims.

Okay, so that's philosophy, but why should we care? Ah, the question of the hour. The question that probably drove you to either read this introduction or not. The answer is an easy one: **Philosophy has taught us how to think.** Not only do the philosophers tell us **what** to think, they teach us **how** to think. The study of the history of philosophy is not just a study of the history of ideas, but rather the history of our own cognition, our own **way of thinking.** Our modern reliance on empirical data and experimentation, as well as our faith in the reliance on logical argument to prove guilt or innocence, are all the fruits of the philosophical seeds planted centuries upon centuries ago. Our ideas influence our cognition, and the study of the historical development of those ideas, that is to say, the study of philosophy, is like stepping into the mind of an ancient author, whose insights have created the ideas that we hold, the method by which we hold them, and even the sound of our deepest, inner voice.

Take the difference between two major existentialists of the twentieth century, Sartre and Camus. Camus' famous novella, *The Stranger*, explores the existentialist angst of the human condition by illuminating the life of its protagonist, who is a "stranger" in every respect: separate from the land and other people. He represents the profoundly isolated condition of the individual. But while literary creations of this sort may explore or expose certain philosophical theories, they are not in themselves a product of philosophy. On the other hand, Sartre, while he also wrote plays and novels, is considered to be the most substantial philosopher of the two for not only are his existentialist theories exposed in his literary works, but these ideas are specified and completely developed in his philosophical treatises, where he seeks to prove that his beliefs are correct.

It will become evident through this exploration that certain groups of philosophers focus on different aspects of general philosophical practice. Some are primarily moral or political theorists while others contribute their genius to the study of epistemology and metaphysics. It will also be made evident that philosophy is an all-encompassing discipline, and as the worlds of facts, society, and politics change, philosophical discourse changes with it. For example, philosophers of the early modern period (such as Hobbes and Descartes) sought to incorporate and understand the philosophical implications of the scientific discoveries of Galileo and Copernicus, while contemporary philosophers seek to incorporate and understand the philosophical implications of all relevant scientific study (such as cloning or space travel) done today. But more than just incorporating scientific evidence into his philosophy, the philosopher inevitably concerns himself with the issues and problems of his time. The study of the history of philosophy is interesting in this way, for while the philosopher *responds to his contemporary world, he must also respond to the philosophical arguments and assertions of the past, as well as to the fundamental problems of philosophy, problems that, since the time of the ancient Greeks, have challenged and inspired all philosophers, no matter what the era.*

In this book, we will uncover this history of ideas by looking at some of the great philosophers over the past two thousand years. Each chapter will consist of a brief description of their lives and a brief discussion of their major ideas. For the philosophical novice, I have included a common metaphor to be used as an explanation tool in each chapter. In order to help the reader differentiate between philosophers, the recurring metaphor of **Bessie the Cow** will be used. Hopefully, she will be as useful as she is anthropomorphic. So, let's get this party started!

CHAPTER ONE

# Thales and the Pre-Socratics

**(640–469 B.C.)**

- **Tried to describe the nature of the universe**
- **Backed their assertions with argument**
- **Raised the basic problems of philosophy**

The long Western tradition of philosophical enquiry began on the soil of ancient Greece. There are a wide variety of "pre-Socratic" philosophers asserting many unique philosophical positions. But they had one thing in common, that is, philosophy.

The "father" of philosophy is Thales (640-550 B.C.). Not only did he supposedly predict an eclipse, a significant scientific contribution at the time, but he is famous for his assertion that the fundamental principle of the universe was water. That is to say, that the "stuff" of which our universe is composed is fundamentally a derivation or product of water. In this assertion, philosophy and science begin. While ancient folks could predict the cosmos as well, and had many theories about the universe, they were not philosophers. For Thales found it necessary to do two things:

1) Attribute his conclusions of the universe to nothing other than the universe itself (i.e., not the gods).
2) Provide an argument as justification for his views.

These are the tenets that separate philosophy from other disciplines, tenets that still apply today.

## Problems and Concerns of the Pre-Socratics

With Thales' claim, we see the first problem of philosophy, the **Problem of Substance**. That is to say, what are the fundamental principles in the world? This effort to determine the "substances" and principles of existence will later be called metaphysics. Thales claimed this fundamental principle of life was water, but his successor, Anaximenes, would claim that the origin of all things was air.

Another ancient concern was that of **being** and **change**. That is to say, how can being and change exist together? If being persists, and beings change (come into being and pass away), how could being persist and not persist? (Ah, those wacky Greeks.)

This metaphysical problem will be taken up by almost every philosopher in the millennia to come.

So, what were some of the "pre-Socratic" answers?

## The Eleatics and "Pure Being"

One system to explain the apparent contradiction between change and being was the philosophy of the Eleatics. These philosophers shared the common claim that there was a changeless, permanent principle of all things. This is the concept of "pure being." It encompasses both the material and the spiritual. Parmenides, a famous Eleatic, claimed that **being** is both infinite space and thought. This is the one principle without parts and lacking nothing at all. Thus, there is one ultimate reality or ultimate principle (being) underlying the existence of every particular, finite thing.

While Thales was more interested in the fundamental "stuff" or "thing" in the physical world, the Eleatics sought an ultimate principle to account for both mental and physical life.

## Heraclitus and Universal Change

Contrary to the Eleatic view that matter is "fixed" and changeless, Heraclitus can be called the "philosopher of universal flux." Everything is in motion and is constantly changing. These bodies are contraries or opposites, and the world is the ceaseless, yet orderly, process of their motion. For Heraclitus, the essence of **being is becoming.** But what are these material bodies made of? Heraclitus claims that the fundamental "stuff" that manifests itself in bodies that undergo change is **fire**.

Out of these explanations of **change and being** comes the idea that there can be continuous change in the "material stuff" of the world while there can be a kind of permanence in the essence or properties of those material things.

## The Relative Change of Absolute Parts

Some "pre-Socratic" philosophers, such as Empedocles, claimed that the universe is made up of the four elements of fire, earth, air, and water, and the world can be explained by these elements in motion. Others, such as Democritus (and the Atomists), claim that there are tiny bits of fundamental "stuff" or atoms that cannot be seen but which serve as the basic building blocks of everything. (Sound similar to modern scientific theories? It should!)

Thus, for most of the philosophers living before Socrates the concerns were how to explain the natural world, and discover the fundamental principles that operate within it. But not for all of them. **Enter the Sophists!**

## The Sophists

The Sophists were the first to make philosophy a practical occupation. They were less concerned about concepts like **being** and more concerned about teaching the art of argumentation to make a few bucks on the side. Each man has his own perceptions and no other person can really decipher which one of those perceptions is "true," said the Sophists. There are no ultimate principles of the universe that can be discovered, and all philosophers who try to discover them are essentially wasting their time. Knowledge is derived from the senses and they do not reveal the true, the universal, or the immutable in the world. The Sophists developed the doctrine of worldly success and satisfaction as the goal of human life.

According to the Sophists, we can never know the "true" or the "good," for "man is the measure of all things." In the philosophical tradition before Socrates, philosophical views had differed tremendously.

However, it is the reliance on logical argument that made philosophy what it is and not something else. Philosophy had gone from explaining the principles of the universe to denying that anything true can be known at all. What was philosophy to do?

The Sophists were at the height of their popularity in Socrates' day. Would he accept philosophy as a guide to material success by way of learning tricky and persuasive arguments? You guessed it . . . hell, no!

### Bessie the Cow

A farmer, who owns Bessie the cow, sells her milk, which turns out to be poisonous and many people die. She continues to sell it anyway. Is she wrong for doing so? According to the Sophists, there is no absolute morality and, if there is, human beings have no knowledge of it. Billy says selling the milk is wrong and Barry says it's right. Really, all we have to go by are the opinions of men, and those opinions differ from person to person.

**Thales:**

*The principle of all things is water; all comes from water, and to water all things return.*

**Anaximenes:**

*Just as our souls, being air, hold us together, so do breath and air encompass the world.*

**Empedocles:**

*God is a circle whose center is everywhere and whose circumference is nowhere.*

*What is lawful is not binding only on some and not binding on others. Lawfulness extends everywhere, through the wide-ruling air and the boundless light of the sky.*

## Democritus:

*It is better to correct your own faults than those of another.*

*Good means not merely not to do wrong, but rather not to desire to do wrong.*
*There are many who know many things, yet are lacking in wisdom.*

*You can tell the man who rings true from the man who rings false, not by his deeds alone, but also his desires.*

*My enemy is not the man who wrongs me, but the man who means to wrong me.*

*Men have made an idol of luck as an excuse for their own thoughtlessness.*

*Now, as of old, the gods give men all good things, excepting only those that are baneful and injurious and useless. These, now as of old, are not gifts of the gods: Men stumble into them themselves because of their own blindness and folly.*

*Throw moderation to the winds, and the greatest pleasures bring the greatest pains.*

*I would rather discover one scientific fact than become King of Persia.*

*Nothing exists except atoms and empty space; everything else is opinion.*

**Parmenides:**

*The only ways of inquiry there are for thinking: The One, that it is and that it is not possible for it not to be, the other, that it is not and it is necessary for it not to be, this I point out to you to be a path completely unlearnable, for neither may you know that which is not, nor may you declare it.*

**Heraclitus:**

*All Things are an exchange for fire and fire for all things, as goods for gold and gold for goods.*

*The thunderbolt steers all things.*

*War is the father of all and king of all, and some he shows as gods, others as humans; some he makes slaves, others free.*

*Disease makes health pleasant and good, hunger satiety, weariness rest.*

*Upon those who step into the same rivers, different and again different waters flow.*

*The road going up and the road down are one and the same.*

**Protagoras (Sophist):**

*Man is the measure of all things—of all things that are, that they are, and of things that are not, that they are not.*

*To make a weaker argument the stronger.*

*There are two sides to every question.*

**Antiphon (Sophist):**

*Time is a thought or a measure, not a reality.*

CHAPTER TWO

# Socrates

**(469–400 B.C.)**

- **Made humans the subject of philosophy**
- **Asserted knowledge to be the goal of human life**
- **Paid the ultimate price for his beliefs**

Socrates is the big kahuna of philosophers—he is known by all as the "font of great wisdom," and is often regarded with a certain amount of mystique, because he never bothered to document his famous moral and metaphysical ideas. Instead he took them to the streets. His very name conjures up images of a caring, courageous, and uncommonly clever man conversing with his fellow Athenians in the *agora* (marketplace).

All we know about Socrates comes from the works of his most famous disciple, Plato, who faithfully recorded his teachings for posterity, not to mention all those Philosophy 101 classes.

Socrates was born in Athens, the son of a respected sculptor. This respectability earned Socrates the right to the best education Athens had to offer—that is to say, he learned everything there was to know at that time about arithmetic, geometry, classical Greek poetry, and astronomy. He also served as a *hoplite*, a foot soldier in the army. His bravery and endurance at the siege of Potidaea during the battle of Delirum were greatly celebrated by his friends and fellow Athenians. However, it would not be his bravery in battle but his beliefs and teachings that would eventually cost him his life.

Socrates talked with anyone who would listen, regardless of their age or social status. His enemies referred to his method of teaching as "prattling on end." However, history would not judge these conversations as endless prattle—but rather as a form of philosophical inquiry called "The Socratic Method."

Socrates himself called his method *telenchus*, roughly translatable as "cross examination." He never took a position himself; instead, he insisted on questioning the assertions and beliefs of others. This cross examination revealed the contradictions in their arguments, thus proving their positions wrong. Socrates' only stance: That he was sure of his ignorance.

The "wise man of the agora," as he was known, felt it was his religious duty to relieve Athenians of their false and unquestioned beliefs, whether they liked it or not. When Chaerephon consulted the most important oracle in Athenian faith, the oracle of Delphi, about Socrates, he asked whether there was any man wiser than Socrates. The priestess responded that there was not. Upon hearing this, Socrates was encouraged to pursue his philosophical lifestyle, despite his detractors—a fateful decision, as it turns out.

In the year 400 B.C., Socrates was indicted for "corrupting the youth of Athens." He was also accused of not worshipping the state gods. Socrates was found guilty and convicted. Apparently, the penalty for philosophical discussion in Athens was death by hemlock (poison). Given the opportunity to escape his sentence, Socrates courageously refused to flee. As Plato put it, Socrates would rather die in Athens than live outside it.

We remember Socrates not for his answers but for his questions. Unsatisfied with the answers that religion, astronomy, and mathematics could provide, Socrates encouraged his fellow Athenians to question their gods, their values, and themselves. What is justice? What is beautiful? What is good? These are the questions that Socrates encouraged all of us to ask, questions that are as relevant today as they were in his own time. Thanks to Socrates, philosophical inquiry now addresses human concerns, values, and dreams. He gave us a new means to seek the truth—and in doing so made philosophy into a true art form. Pretty good for a guy who claimed to know nothing at all.

*I am the wisest man alive, for I know one thing, and that is that I know nothing.*

*Be slow to fall into friendship, but when thou art in, continue firm and constant.*

*Only the extremely ignorant or the extremely intelligent can resist change.*

*The shortest and surest way to live with honor in the world is to be in reality what we would appear to be; all human virtues increase and strengthen themselves by the practice and experience of them.*

*True knowledge exists in knowing that you know nothing.*

*An unexamined life is not worth living.*

*Virtue does not come from wealth, but wealth, and every other good thing which men have comes from virtue.*

*Think not those faithful who praise all thy words and actions; but those who kindly reprove thy faults.*

*They are not only idle who do nothing, but they are idle also who might be better employed.*

*Some have courage in pleasures, and some in pains: some in desires, and some in fears, and some are cowards under the same conditions.*

*Man's life is like a drop of dew on a leaf.*

*Let him that would move the world, first move himself.*

*I cannot teach anybody anything. I can only make them think.*

*By all means marry. If you get a good wife, you'll be happy. If you get a bad one, you'll become a philosopher . . . and that is a good thing for any man.*

*Nothing is to be preferred before justice.*

*Beauty is a short-lived tyranny.*

*Be as you wish to seem.*

*He is richest who is content with the least, for content is the wealth of nature.*

*To find yourself, think for yourself.*

*My belief is that to have no wants is divine.*

*Thou shouldst eat to live; not live to eat.*

*There is only one good, knowledge, and one evil, ignorance.*

*I am not an Athenian or a Greek, but a citizen of the world.*

*Envy is the ulcer of the soul.*

*I do nothing but go about persuading you all, old and young alike, not to take thought for your persons or your properties, but and chiefly to care about the greatest improvement of the soul. I tell you that virtue is not given by money, but that from virtue comes money and every other good of man, public as well as private. This is my teaching, and if this is the doctrine which corrupts the youth, I am a mischievous person.*

CHAPTER THREE

# Plato

**(427–347 B.C.)**

- Reason and the soul are immortal
- The physical world is not the true reality
- Ideas (forms) are changeless, eternal, and exist in a separate world

Socrates was to Plato what Dr. Dre is to Eminem, a teacher and mentor. Eminem learned from Dre like Plato learned from Socrates, and in both cases the protégé took the art form in an entirely new direction. Much like his teacher, Plato posed philosophical questions that philosophers still tackle today. However, Plato concerned himself with the fundamental "stuff" of the universe and the foundation of human knowledge. If Socrates took philosophy to the streets, Plato took philosophy back up to the sky.

Plato was born to wealthy Athenian parents. He was a gifted child, and thus eventually became Socrates' favorite pupil and greatest champion. When he was forty, he founded the famed Academy school, and he lectured and wrote there until his death.

Plato accepted the Socratic method of learning and built upon it, developing a complete theory of the universe. His dialogues not only reveal to us the Socratic way of thinking, they help us discover more abstract truths.

## Plato's Big Idea #1: The Form

Plato's big idea, actually, **is** the idea, or as he calls it, the "form." According to Plato, the "real" stuff in the universe is the "form" or "essence" of the object, not the particular manifestation of it in front of our eyes. The physical world and objects around us are just mere copies of these forms, the form being "what makes that particular thing what it is and not something else." In other words, its essence. Forms are the only "real" and enduring substances. These substances exist in a world apart from human perception. What we perceive through our senses is only a copy of the real form. The form itself is comprehended through our exercise of reason.

In other words, Bessie the Cow is not real—it's her universal form as a cow that is real. It is only when we use reason to deduce the form of "cowness" that we come to the realization of the true reality. This pertains to moral notions as well. I know it sounds funny, but Plato isn't exactly a moron, so hear out his argument. A particular act is *good* because there is something in the act itself that makes it such. This "thing" is the universal ideal of "goodness." Moral notions are not considered good simply because they produce desirable results, but because they conform to this universal ideal of "goodness."

## Plato's Big Idea #2: The Rational Man

The theory of forms is the key to understanding Plato's Rational Man. Because what we perceive is not real, we cannot trust our senses, and must therefore rely upon reason.

Plato contends that we gain knowledge only through the exercise of Reason. With reason, we can comprehend the eternal and the changeless, whereas our senses will lead us astray, into the world of copies or imperfect imitations. Just as forms are changeless and eternal, reason is eternal. And just as the cosmos is ordered (based on this world of forms), so is the human soul. As humans, we should override our senses and desires and let the higher function of the soul (reason) run the show. Do this, and you become Plato's Rational Man.

The Rational Man is eternal—as the eternal forms are immortal, so is the Rational Man. Like the eternal nature of the "forms," the rational part of the human soul has an eternal or immortal status. Human souls transmigrate in an eternal cycle of life and death. For example, when Plato dies, the rational part of his soul will be reborn in Aristotle. Each human being's learning experience is essentially a rediscovery of eternal truths.

Plato doesn't stop there. He takes his passion for reason and form and applies it to his political philosophy as well. In *The Republic*, Plato argues that just as the good life is a life ruled by reason, so should the state be run by the Rational Man. Who are these rational men? You guessed it, the philosophers. Hence the term "philosopher king." Plato argues that philosophers are less concerned with personal desire and can comprehend the universality of the whole society and its needs, and therefore make the best kings.

Take a look around: Now you tell me, don't we need a philosopher king?

*Philosophy is the highest music.*

*Death is not the worst that can happen to men.*

*No human thing is of serious importance.*

*If women are expected to do the same work as men, we must teach them the same things.*

*Ignorance, the root and the stem of every evil.At the touch of love, everyone becomes a poet.*

*Never discourage anyone . . . who continually makes progress, no matter how slow.*

*The price good men pay for indifference to public affairs is to be ruled by evil men.*

*There is no such thing as a lover's oath.*

*Wise men talk because they have something to say; fools, because they have to say something.*

*You can discover more about a person in an hour of play than in a year of conversation.*

*No evil can happen to a good man, either in life or after death.*

*You cannot conceive the many without the one.*

*False words are not only evil in themselves, but they infect the soul with evil.*

*The greatest penalty of evildoing—namely, to grow into the likeness of bad men.*

*You are young, my son, and, as the years go by, time will change and even reverse many of your present opinions. Refrain therefore awhile from setting yourself up as a judge of the highest matters.*

*Bodily exercise, when compulsory, does no harm to the body; but knowledge which is acquired under compulsion obtains no hold on the mind.*

*Everything that deceives may be said to enchant.*

*He who is of calm and happy nature will hardly feel the pressure of age, but to him who is of an opposite disposition youth and age are equally a burden.*

*The beginning is the most important part of the work.*

*The direction in which education starts a man will determine his future life.*

*The people have always some champion whom they set over them and nurse into greatness . . . This and no other is the root from which a tyrant springs; when he first appears, he is a protector.*

*The soul of man is immortal and imperishable.*

*Wealth is the parent of luxury and indolence, and poverty of meanness and viciousness, and both of discontent.*

*A dog has the soul of the philosopher.*

CHAPTER FOUR

# Aristotle

**(384–322 B.C.)**

- Founder of scientific logic, biology, and classical literary criticism
- Asserted teleological conception of nature
- Looked to the particular objects themselves to understand our comprehension of them

If someone shouted, "Will the real slim ancient Greek philosopher please stand up?" Aristotle would no doubt rise to his feet. It's not just that Aristotle is an essential figure in the evolution of Western thought. For millennia, he defined it. Western civilization itself is "Aristotelian," at least until the seventeenth century.

Aristotle was born fourteen years after the death of Socrates at Stagirus, a Greek colony on the coast of Thrace. His father was court physician to the King of Macedon. Although his father died when he was still a boy, Aristotle would maintain a long and important relationship with the Macedonian court. At age seventeen, Aristotle was sent to Athens to study. He got a pretty good education there. After all, Plato was his teacher! There, in Plato's famed school, the Academy, Aristotle listened to Plato's lectures for a period of twenty years. During his later years at the Academy, Aristotle began giving his own lectures, mainly on the subject of rhetoric.

Plato wasn't his only high-profile pal. Thanks to his association with the Macedonian court, Aristotle became a tutor to a thirteen-year-old prince named Alexander. As in, Alexander the Great! After Plato's death, Aristotle, although certainly qualified, did not succeed Plato to head the Academy. His divergence from Platonic thought had become too great.

Upon the sudden death of Alexander, and the subsequent removal of the Pro-Macedonian government in 323 B.C., Aristotle fled from a charge of impiety placed upon him by the new elite. Referring to Socrates' death, Aristotle told his fellow Athenians that he was leaving Athens, in order that they "might not sin against philosophy twice." He died about a year later in Chalcis.

## Aristotle's Big Idea #1: Matter and Form

For Aristotle, matter and form are both "real" things. For example, Bessie the Cow is not seen as a mere copy of the Platonic universal form of "cowness" (i.e., what it is to be a cow). The particular matter (Bessie the Cow) is understood as *potentiality* while form is understood as *actuality*. Thus, while the universal form of "cowness" is separable from the particular cow itself in thought, it is not separable in ontology (reality). In other words, the form of "cowness" does not exist in another "world of forms," but exists within Bessie herself.

## Aristotle's Big Idea #2: The Four Causes

While studying nature, Aristotle was interested in the "causes" of each living thing. He identified "four causes" at work in the natural world. The four causes are the material, efficient, formal, and final. In the case of a stuffed cow, the material cause would be the cotton and cloth, the formal cause would be its blueprint or designated form, the efficient cause would be the worker who made it, and the final cause would be the rural child who would play with it.

But Aristotle contends that this process actually is responsible for the development of a real cow like our Bessie. The material cause being the matter out of which she is made, the formal cause being her genetic blueprint, the efficient cause being the minute biological processes, and the final cause being the aim of developing into adulthood. In this view, the purpose of a baby cow is to be an adult cow. The regularity at which things develop in nature led Aristotle to believe that "nature does not act out of arbitrariness." Nature works for a purpose or to fulfill an aim. If matter is indeterminate as Aristotle claims, something must cause it to develop into a recognizable form. The fact that this occurs with such regularity and predictability suggests that the development of each organism (like that of human artifacts) is driven by inherent purpose or towards an ultimate aim. This is called *Aristotelian teleology*.

This idea of purposefulness applies to man as well. The purpose of all particular human desires is ultimately happiness. If one becomes a stockbroker to make money, one thinks that money will eventually make one happy. For what good would it be if it doesn't? But only virtue (proper action through reason), according to Aristotle, makes men truly happy. The attainment of happiness through the practice of reason is "the highest good."

## Aristotle's Big Idea #3: The Syllogism

The invention of the logical syllogism is the tool Aristotle gives us to practice our reason and to discover truth. An example of a syllogism is the following:

All men are mortal
Socrates is a man
Therefore, Socrates is mortal.

Aristotle's conception of the causes at work in nature went virtually unchallenged in the West for over a thousand years. In addition, his scientific logic and biological studies set the foundation for both these thriving disciplines. Indeed, he was the King of Big Ideas—as his dicta on the cathartic aspect of tragedy is accepted and discussed by literary critics and scholars to this day. More than just a contributory figure in the history of ideas, Aristotle's philosophy has embedded itself in our understanding of Western intellectual culture. But don't be jealous, your teachers weren't half as good as his.

*Plato is dear to me, but dearer still is truth.*

*Man is by nature a political animal.*

*All paid jobs absorb and degrade the mind.*

*Education is the best provision for the journey to old age.*

*Happiness depends upon ourselves.*

*It is in justice that the ordering of society is centered.*

*It is the mark of an educated mind to be able to entertain a thought without accepting it.*

*Pleasure in the job puts perfection in the work.*

*Poverty is the parent of revolution and crime.*

*The only stable state is the one in which all men are equal before the law.*

*It is not always the same thing to be a good man and a good citizen.*

*Misfortune shows those who are not really friends.*

*Hope is a waking dream.*

*All men by nature desire knowledge.*

*It is possible to fail in many ways . . . while to succeed is possible only in one way.*

*One swallow does not make a summer.*

*We make war that we may live in peace.*

*In all things of nature there is something of the marvelous.*

*It is the nature of desire not to be satisfied, and most men live only for the gratification of it.*

*Law is order, and good law is good order.*

*Nature does nothing uselessly.*

*The basis of a democratic state is liberty.*

*They should rule who are able to rule best.*

*Evil draws men together.*

*It is simplicity that makes the uneducated more effective than the educated when addressing popular audiences.*

CHAPTER FIVE

# St. Augustine

**(A.D. 354–430)**

- Asserted the first "philosophy of history"
- Championed Faith over Reason
- Invented the genre of introspective autobiography

The writings of St. Augustine are both intensely personal and spiritual as well as philosophically profound. Living and writing during the fall of the great Roman Empire, it is no surprise that the focus of his philosophical work is not on the relationship of individual citizens to the political State, but on the relationship of human beings with God.

Born to a middle-class family in modern-day Algeria, St. Augustine's spiritual upbringing reflects the multiculturalism and diversity found within the Roman Empire at the time. His father, a small farmer and government official, was a pagan, while his mother was a Christian. He was very close to his mother early on in his life, and eventually he would adopt her religion as well. But as a seventeen-year-old young man studying rhetoric in Carthage, he rejected Christianity and embraced the philosophies of the Greeks as well as a variety of pagan religions, including Manichaeanism (a dualistic religious philosophy taught by the Persian prophet Manes). Over the course of the next several years, St. Augustine was a wild and crazy guy, living a life of sexual indulgence that he details in his famous autobiographical work "Confessions."

Ultimately, St. Augustine grew restless. His spirit starved for meaning, he turned away from his self-described "life of sin." He was baptized Christian in A.D. 387—and was later ordained in the Christian community at Hippo, where he eventually served as Bishop until his death.

As Aristotle had a profound effect on the Christian philosopher Aquinas, so did Plato on St. Augustine. He accepted the Platonic notion of the universe, in that the world of experience, time, and space, are less "real" than the "world of ideas or forms." But the eternal reality of forms does not exist in a Platonic "world of forms," but are contained within the "mind of God." However, for St. Augustine the "realm of God" replaces Plato's "realm of forms." St. Augustine also agrees with the Platonic notion that there is no "pure" evil in the universe. There is only "pure" good—because God is all-powerful and all-good. Evil is just the absence of good—as dark is the absence of light. Bad actions are simply those actions where there is no goodness.

## St. Augustine's Big Idea: Faith Rules Reason

St. Augustine spiritualized Reason. God is the author of Reason; He gives it to us so that we might better understand ourselves and God. Knowledge of the Self and of God become the important exercise of Reason, over and above Plato's concern for human social organization.

According to St. Augustine, God gave us free will, and free will is necessary to make moral decisions. God is an omniscient being who knows every decision we will ever make. Thus, when we make decisions, especially moral ones, we cannot just exercise Reason without referring to God. Just as evil is the absence of good, so are immoral decisions that are made in the absence of God. Immorality results when we fail to allow God's grace to guide our behavior.

In St. Augustine's most famous work, *The City of God*, he describes history as the purposeful linear process from creation to consummation and final judgment. As human beings, we should be creating the "city of God," not "the city of Man."

Augustine is the bridge between Christian thought and the Greek philosophers. It is often said that Augustine "baptized" Plato. He did "spiritualize" philosophy, in that he attributes all human knowledge, human history, and the world itself, to an all powerful, all-loving Christian God. So the next time the nuns catch you reading a copy of Plato, just tell them to remember St. Augustine.

**Bessie Falls from Grace**

When a person decides that cow tipping (knocking over a sleeping cow—a common form of entertainment in areas without adequate theater) is a perfectly legitimate thing to do, he is not using his reason and not living within God's grace. That is, when we think of ourselves instead of God.

*Unless you believe, you will not understand.*

*Better to have loved and lost, than to have never loved at all.*

*Men go abroad to admire the heights of mountains, the mighty billows of the sea, the broad tides of rivers, the compass of the ocean, and the circuits of the stars, and pass themselves by.*

*Patience is the companion of wisdom.*

*Faith is to believe what you do not see; the reward of this faith is to see what you believe.*

*A thing is not necessarily true because badly uttered, nor false because spoken magnificently.*

*To wisdom belongs the intellectual apprehension of things eternal; to knowledge, the rational apprehension of things temporal.*

*God will not suffer man to have the knowledge of things to come; for if he had prescience of his prosperity he would be careless; and understanding of his adversity he would be senseless.*

*We make ourselves a ladder out of our vices if we trample the vices themselves underfoot.*

*Miracles are not contrary to nature, but only contrary to what we know about nature.*

*Conscience and reputation are two things. Conscience is due to yourself, reputation to your neighbor.*

*Hear the other side.*

*O Lord, help me to be pure, but not yet.*

*The argument is at an end.*

*I was in love with loving.*

*Order your soul; reduce your wants; live in charity; associate in Christian community; obey the laws; trust in Providence.*

*Pray as though everything depended on God. Work as though everything depended on you.*

*Since love grows within you, so beauty grows. For love is the beauty of the soul.*

*The people who remained victorious were less like conquerors than conquered.*

CHAPTER SIX

# Thomas Aquinas

**(1225–1274)**

- Merged Christian theology and philosophy
- Provided rational proofs for the existence of God
- Separated Faith from Reason

Aquinas is "the Man" of medieval philosophy. During the High Middle Ages, the works of Aristotle and the Greeks were rediscovered in the West, even though they didn't fit well with the church dogma of the day. Before Aquinas, the tradition of medieval Christian philosophy had its influence in the neo-Platonic Augustinian tradition, but as Plato inspired Augustine, Aristotle inspired Aquinas. Aquinas sought to synthesize Aristotle and Christianity. This synthesis is often referred to as the Aristotelian/Scholastic tradition. In some sense, as Augustine "spiritualized" Plato, Aquinas sought to rationalize religious belief. He sought to prove the validity of those beliefs through the power of rational philosophical argument.

Born to a noble family in Roccasecca, Italy, Aquinas joined the Dominican order while studying philosophy at Naples. But his family wasn't too fond of his philosophical pursuits, and his brothers seized him and held him captive for about a year in their family home. However, he would not give up, and his family finally let him go. The order sent him to Paris and Cologne, where he was exposed to Aristotle. He spent the rest of his life as a teacher and scholar; his reputation earned him the title of "angelic doctor."

## Aquinas's Big Idea: Reason vs. Faith

According to Aquinas, there are two types of knowledge. One is the knowledge of the spiritual, which we learn through our faith in God. The other type we learn through Reason.

Aquinas distinguishes between Reason and faith; yet he also uses Reason to prove faith. He gives us several rational "proofs" of God. His starting point is the Aristotelian notion of the necessity of an "unmoved mover." The fact that the world is in motion means that something must first have caused this motion. That first cause is God. For example, the fact that there is a particular cow named Bessie means that something

must have "caused" it. If you trace back all the Bessies that have been created over thousands of years, eventually one has to come to the conclusion that there was a first cause of the universe. Something must have set something in motion for there to be motion
at all.

Aquinas contends that God is not just a "first cause" of motion, but also a moral Christian. The very fact that human beings have moral Ideals means that there must be some standard of moral Ideal in the universe. These standards are not Plato's "forms in the sky," but God.

While faith and Reason provide different means of finding the truth, Aquinas tells us that revelation is the more important. Born of the mysterious nature of the spirit, revelation comes to us through faith. To concern ourselves with the spirit alone is adequate for a good life. However, Aquinas challenges those of us with an extraordinary capacity for Reason (like himself) to use this gift to understand the world that God has bestowed on us. While Reason is a different source of knowledge than revelation, both ultimately rest on the one supreme and absolute truth, that is, God.

Aquinas always walked a tightrope between acceptance and rejection from the religious figures and institutions of his day. But eventually his efforts to meld Aristotelian philosophy and Christian thought were successful. He was canonized as a Catholic Saint by Pope John XXII in

1323, and his philosophy was accepted as the official philosophy of the Catholic church by Pope Leo XIII in the nineteenth century.

Whenever Aquinas's name comes up and you want to be able to speak intelligently about his philosophy, just remember, God is really important to him.

*Good can exist without evil, whereas evil cannot exist without good.*
*Beware the man of one book.*

*Perfection of moral virtue does not wholly take away the passions, but regulates them.*

*Three things are necessary for the salvation of man: To know what he ought to believe; to know what he ought to desire; and to know what he ought to do.*

*Love takes up where knowledge ends.*

*There is nothing on this earth like a true friend.*

*Because of the diverse conditions of humans, it happens that some acts are virtuous to some people, as appropriate and suitable to them, while the same acts are immoral for others, as inappropriate to them.*

*The highest manifestation of life consists in this: that a being governs its own actions.*

*A thing which is always subject to the direction of another is somewhat of a dead thing.*

*In order for a war to be just, three things are necessary. First, the authority of the sovereign . . . Secondly, a just cause . . . Thirdly, a rightful intention.*

*Those who are more adapted to the active life can prepare themselves for contemplation in the practice of the active life, while those who are more adapted to the contemplative life can take upon themselves the works of the active life so as to become yet more apt for contemplation.*

*Friendship is the source of the greatest pleasures, and without friends even the most agreeable pursuits become tedious.*

*Clearly the person who accepts the Church as an infallible guide will believe whatever the Church teaches.*

*Human salvation demands the divine disclosure of truths surpassing reason.*

*That the saints may enjoy their beatitude and the grace of God more abundantly they are permitted to see the punishment of the damned in hell.*

*If forgers and malefactors are put to death by the secular power, there is much more reason for excommunicating and even putting to death one convicted of heresy.*

*As regards the individual nature, woman is defective and misbegotten, for the active power of the male seed tends to the production of a perfect likeness in the masculine sex; while the production of a woman comes from defect in the active power.*

*A man has free choice to the extent that he is rational.*

CHAPTER SEVEN

# René Descartes

**(1596–1650)**

- **Father of modern philosophy**
- **Asserted mechanistic view of Nature**
- **Mind and body as distinct substances**

Descartes is the undisputed "father" of modern philosophy. Thanks to his brilliant inquiries into the foundation and method of philosophy, a new intellectualism for a new Europe was born.

Descartes was born the son of a noble family at La Haye, in the Touraine province of France. Educated in the great Jesuit tradition at La Fleche and Poiters, he had a gift for mathematics; his contribution to geometry in particular is as widely esteemed now as then. However, driven to discover life and truth on his own, he left his studies to travel extensively. He even served for a brief time in the military with Prince Maurice of Holland.

Although he recounts meeting many interesting people and engaging in many adventures during that time, Descartes never ceased to ponder the ageless questions of philosophy—and eventually moved to Holland. He lived in seclusion, moving often to maintain his privacy. There he developed his philosophy—a gift greater and more memorable than his contributions to science and geometry.

Galileo and Copernicus had challenged the classic Aristotelian and Christian concepts of the universe. Their discoveries had revolutionized the way in which the universe was to be understood. The birth of modern science depicted the world as unmysterious bits of matter performing predictable physical operations. What basis could there be now for a true understanding of reality? Many thinkers of his day claimed there was no such basis, and that neither the sense nor reason could suffice for absolute knowledge. But not good ol' Descartes.

Descartes assumes nothing about the world. He only decides that something is "real" when he can clearly and distinctly comprehend that it is so. He calls into question the reality of both the mind and the body, that is, reason and nature. This is often called "hyperbolic doubt."

## Descartes' Big Idea #1: "I think therefore I am"

Descartes proves the reality of the mind first by stating that something must be doing all this doubting. As his famous maxim asserts, "I think therefore I am." He also claims that "I am a thinking thing." Thinking is our essence, and thus our mind (reason) is distinct from our body (nature). This is known as Cartesian Dualism.

## Descartes' Big Idea #2: God As Basis for the Reality of the External World

Descartes provides proofs not just for his own existence as a "thinking thing," but also for the existence of God and the world around him. Most important is his proof of the existence of God. One proof Descartes gives to prove God's existence is that as a "thinking thing" he has ideas. One idea he has is that of a perfectly good and absolutely powerful God. Descartes claims that nothing except God could give him this idea. The next claim is that as God is supremely good, he cannot be a deceiver. God would therefore not deceive me. It follows that my belief in an external world based on my "clear and distinct" apprehension of geometric forms or "pure extension" could not be false, for it would require God to be a deceiver.

While Descartes accepted the skeptical claim that our human senses do not present the world as it actually exists, he also says that human knowledge of "pure extension" is possible. This external world of extension is absolutely distinct from the world of the mind. While attributes such as colors and smells exist only in the mind of the perceiver, there are things outside the mind that can be mathematically determined.

## Descartes' Big Idea #3: Matter in Motion

Furthermore, based on the scientific discoveries of his day, Descartes denied the Aristotelian concept of final causation and teleology in Nature. Natural things come into being and pass away simply by efficient causation. Nature is no longer seen as containing inherent purpose and can be understood as simply "matter in motion."

Descartes proved that a demonstrated knowledge of the world, despite our imperfect senses, was indeed possible. He is also remembered for his conception of mind and body as equally "real" but essentially distinct substances. Descartes breaks from the Aristotelian and Scholastic tradition; he single-handedly merges philosophy into the "new" scientific age and saves it from becoming an obsolete form of human enquiry. *I think therefore I am. God is, and he is good. The world is just matter in motion.* Philosophy certainly is a strange discipline.

*I think therefore I am.*

*Divide each difficulty into as many parts as is feasible and necessary to resolve it.*

*It is not enough to have a good mind; the main thing is to use it well.*

*To know what people really think, pay regard to what they do, rather than what they say.*

*Each problem that I solved became a rule, which served afterwards to solve other problems.*

*Perfect numbers like perfect men are very rare.*

*The two operations of our understanding, intuition and deduction, on which alone we have said we must rely in the acquisition of knowledge.*

*Except our own thoughts, there is nothing absolutely in our power.*

*When I consider this carefully, I find not a single property which with certainty separates the waking state from the dream. How can you be certain that your whole life is not a dream?*

*I concluded that I might take as a general rule the principle that all things which we very clearly and obviously conceive are true: only observing, however, that there is some difficulty in rightly determining the objects which we distinctly conceive.*

*You just keep pushing. You just keep pushing. I made every mistake that could be made. But I just kept pushing.*

*If I found any new truths in the sciences, I can say that they follow from, or depend on, five or six principal problems which I succeeded in solving and which I regard as so many battles where the fortunes of war were on my side.*

*If we possessed a thorough knowledge of all the parts of the seed of any animal (e.g. man), we could from that alone, by reasons entirely mathematical and certain, deduce the whole conformation and figure of each of its members, and, conversely if we knew several peculiarities of this conformation, we would from those deduce the nature of its seed.*

*It is only prudent never to place complete confidence in that by which we have even once been deceived.*

*One cannot conceive anything so strange and so implausible that it has not already been said by one philosopher or another.*

*The first precept was never to accept a thing as true until I knew it as such without a single doubt.*

*The greatest minds are capable of the greatest vices as well as of the greatest virtues.*

*The long concatenations of simple and easy reasoning which geometricians use in achieving their most difficult demonstrations gave me occasion to imagine that all matters which may enter the human mind were interrelated in the same fashion.*

*Traveling is almost like talking with those of other centuries.*

*It is easy to hate and it is difficult to love. This is how the whole scheme of things works. All good things are difficult to achieve; and bad things are very easy to get.*

*Nothing is more fairly distributed than common sense: No one thinks he needs more of it than he already has.*

*I am indeed amazed when I consider how weak my mind is and how prone to error.*

*If you would be a real seeker after truth, you must at least once in your life doubt, as far as possible, all things.*

*I hope that posterity will judge me kindly, not only as to the things which I have explained, but also to those which I have intentionally omitted so as to leave to others the pleasure of discovery.*

CHAPTER EIGHT

# Thomas Hobbes

**(1588–1679)**

- Human nature is based on self-interest and the desire for power
- The human mind is just motion in the brain
- Humans form society for protection from a "State of Nature"

Thomas Hobbes was one of the greatest political thinkers in the history of philosophy. The son of a clergyman in Wiltshire, England, his childhood was not the happiest. When he was only seven, his father ran off after a brawl with a fellow vicar. Undone by this unexpected course of events, his mother sent poor little Tommy to live with his uncle Francis. He attended private school in Westport until the age of fourteen. By this time, he was already a classics scholar, having successfully translated Euripides' *Medea* from Greek to Latin. Imagine what his SATs would have been! Hobbes went on to graduate from Oxford in 1608 and became the tutor of Lord William Cavendish, a prominent member of the Stuart royal family.

After years of travel and a promotion to secretary, the eleven-year-old Lord Cavendish's sudden death cost Hobbes both a friend and his secretarial post. Hobbes tutored other members of the upper classes and continued translating classics; but it wasn't until he was over forty that he became interested in philosophy. After meeting Galileo in Paris in the 1630s, Hobbes became fascinated with the popular mechanistic understanding of the universe.

After his magnum opus, *Leviathan,* was published in 1651, he returned to England. Reunited with the Cavendish family, Hobbes spent the last few years of his life at their estate. He died at 91.

## Hobbes' Big Idea #1: Divine Right Doesn't Rule

In a time when royalty ruled by divine right, Hobbes developed a secular justification for the modern State. Even though he was a royalist who supported absolute monarchy, he did not believe that a monarch's right to rule was bestowed by God.

## Hobbes' Big Idea #2: Government Rocks

According to Hobbes, human nature is based on self-interest and a continual desire for power. Before government, life was "brutish and short"—think *Lord of the Flies*. This is what he refers to as the "State of Nature." So people entered into a "social contract" with a ruler for protection, thereby creating government. Hobbes is the first in a long line of thinkers who would adopt this "social contract" theory of civilization. Although people consent out of fear, this social contract is the only way to achieve a decent life. The State exists for man and dictates the laws and morals. The commands of the State are supremely good, because they're part of the social contract. In short, we need government, and we need rulers.

## Hobbes' Big Idea #3: Materialism

Hobbes believes that the only universal principle is that of motion. The mind, therefore, is not a "thinking substance," but just movement in the brain. Hobbes takes the "real" to mean only the physical world and not the "ideas" of man. This is the doctrine of philosophical materialism. Man acts by nature from his desires. Man has his essence not as a "thinking thing" but as a machine in motion. Reason is understood to be just a kind of calculating device, a device that relates one thing to another. With Hobbes, reason loses the eternal and divine-like quality that Plato and other philosophers had given it. By asserting this view, Hobbes rejects Plato and Aristotle's idea that government is a result of man's natural social instinct. On the contrary, man's natural instinct is a state of "nature" or "war." Man only enters into a social contract based on the rational necessity for protection against the "state of nature" to which he himself is naturally inclined.

Hobbes takes the scientific view of the world as "matter in motion" that Descartes asserted, and applies this mechanistic conception to human beings. Furthermore, Hobbes provides the first modern secular argument for the legitimacy of government—and manages to validate absolute monarchy at the same time (though he has no philosophical objection to democracy—but considers monarchy more efficient in controlling the warlike inclinations of men). While rulers do not receive their right to rule from God, Hobbes has no problem with a monarch who inherits his position from his parents. Hobbes is still relevant today, even if we would never agree with one's right to rule based on who one's parents were. Wait a minute . . . would we?

*The science which teacheth arts and handicrafts is merely science for the gaining of a living; but the science which teacheth deliverance from worldly existence, is not that the true science?*

*In the first place, I put before a general inclination of all mankind, a perpetual and restless desire of power after power, that ceaseth only in death.*

*In the state of nature, profit is the measure of right.*

*Not believing in force is the same as not believing in gravitation.*

*Science is the knowledge of consequences, and dependence of one fact upon another.*

*Such is the nature of men, that howsoever they may acknowledge many others to be more witty, or more eloquent, or more learned; yet they will hardly believe there be many so wise as themselves.*

*The disembodied spirit is immortal; there is nothing of it that can grow old or die. But the embodied spirit sees death on the horizon as soon as its day dawns.*

*The right of nature . . . is the liberty each man hath to use his own power, as he will himself, for the preservation of his own nature; that is to say, of his own life.*

*For the laws of nature (as justice, equity, modesty, mercy, and in sum, doing to others as we would be done to) of themselves, without the terror of some power to cause them to be observed, are contrary to our natural passions, that carry us to partiality, pride, revenge and the like.*

*The source of every crime is some defect of the understanding; or some error in reasoning; or some sudden force of the passions.*

*Another doctrine repugnant to civil society, is that whatsoever a man does against his conscience, is sin, and it dependeth on the presumptions of making himself judge of good and evil. For a man's conscience and judgment are the same thing, and as the judgment, so also the conscience may be erroneous.*

*Laughter is nothing else but sudden glory arising from some sudden conception of some eminency in ourselves, by comparison with the infirmity of others, or with our own formerly.*

*Corporations are many lesser commonwealths in the bowels of a greater, like worms in the entrails of a natural man.*

*Leisure is the mother of philosophy.*

*Intemperance is naturally punished with diseases; rashness, with mischance; injustice, with violence of enemies; pride, with ruin; cowardice, with oppression; and rebellion, with slaughter.*

*All generous minds have a horror of what are commonly called "Facts."*
*As a draft-animal is yoked in a wagon, even so the spirit is yoked in this body.*

*Appetite, with an opinion of attaining, is called hope; the same, without such opinion, despair.*

*Fear of things invisible is the natural seed of that which everyone in himself calleth religion.*

*Where there is no common power there is no law, where there is no law there is no injustice.*

*Life in this State of Nature is without Art, without letters, without society, and worst of all, continual fear and danger of violent death.*

*Without laws and society, the life of man is solitary, poor, nasty, brutish and short.*

*Good, and evil, are nothing more than names that signify our appetites, and aversions: which in different tempers, and doctrines of men, are different.*

*During the time men live without a common power to keep them all in awe, they are in that condition called war; as if every man, the notions of right and wrong have no place.*

*I am about to take my last voyage. A great leap in the dark.*
*(attributed last words)*

CHAPTER NINE

# Benedict Spinoza

**(1632–1677)**

- Denied final causation even in God
- Asserted unique conception of human freedom
- God as one and only Substance

Not only is Benedict Spinoza crucially important in the developmental history of Western philosophy, he was also a man courageous enough to stand up to his principles, and defend the spirit of philosophy itself. He was the Socrates of modern philosophy.

Born in Holland to exiled Portuguese Jews, Spinoza's father pushed him to become a Rabbi. However, Spinoza found little in Jewish theology that satisfied him. Instead, he turned to the philosophers of the day for guidance—namely Hobbes and Descartes. After renouncing Orthodox Judaism and sticking to his philosophical views whatever the consequence, Spinoza was excommunicated from the Jewish community. He settled in The Hague, making his living by grinding lenses. Although his writings aroused intense interest, they also aroused an even more intense indignation. So strong was this indignation that he was forced to write most of his work under an assumed name. Fiercely dedicated to free philosophical enquiry, Spinoza rejected a prestigious professorship at the University of Heidelberg, which was offered to him on the condition that he remain reasonably orthodox. The last ten years of his life were a period of great production. He died at The Hague from consumption. He was only 45.

## Spinoza's Big Idea #1: God Is Infinite and Perfect

Spinoza is famous for his assertion that "Everything that is, is in God." In an ironic twist of fate he was labeled an atheist for this philosophy, since Spinoza's God (a word he interchanges with "Nature") went against the Judeo-Christian conception of divinity. Spinoza asked: If God is infinite and perfect, how can he act towards an end? According to the philosopher, he cannot.

If God is infinite and perfect, then:

1) God must be everywhere and everything must somehow be in

God. For if God is an infinite substance, there must be no substance other than he.

2) God must act out of necessity and not choice. Thus, he cannot act towards a final goal. For acting towards something indicates a necessary lack of something. If God is lacking something, he cannot be perfect.

Spinoza began with the principles associated with God and followed them to their logical conclusions. His purpose was not to undermine God as infinite, but to undermine the notion of God as a willful, final cause of the world. Like Descartes, Spinoza believed that God must exist, because his essence includes existence.

God, according to Spinoza, is the only "real" substance on earth; a substance of two attributes—thought and extension. Everything—from our thoughts to the material world—is just a tiny expression of one infinite substance (God/Nature).

## Spinoza's Big Idea #2: God Is Not Final Cause

According to Spinoza, God became viewed as "acting towards a specific end" because human beings, finding many things useful in nature, made the logical mistake that this "usefulness" implied its "purposefulness." For example, Bessie the Cow makes good eatin' and gives human beings the protein to survive. She is useful as a food source (sorry, Bessie), but just because she is useful does not mean that she was created specifically and willfully to serve that purpose. This conception of "purposefulness" attributed to God or Nature arose from the logical mistake of attributing "usefulness" as "purposefulness."

## Spinoza's Idea #3: Freedom Is Acting in Accord with One's Nature

Spinoza claims that true freedom is not the ability to "choose" one thing over another (free will), but the ability to act according to one's nature and to act alone. God is free because he is infinite and requires nothing else for his existence. For us humans, freedom consists of understanding our desires and our place in the universe as a cause of God.

Spinoza is not only a great philosopher, but a great man whose life is a testament to the spirit of philosophy itself. Spinoza, I raise my glass to you, sir. Mazel Tov!

*Whatsoever is, is in God, and without God nothing can be, or be conceived.*

*Do not weep; do not wax indignant. Understand.*

*Be not astonished at new ideas; for it is well known to you that a thing does not therefore cease to be true because it is not accepted by many.*

*Peace is not an absence of war, it is a virtue, a state of mind, a disposition for benevolence, confidence, justice.*

*I have made a ceaseless effort not to ridicule, not to bewail, not to scorn human actions, but to understand.*

*He alone is free who lives with free consent under the guidance of reason.*

*There is no hope without fear, and there is no fear without hope.*

*Our actions, that is to say, those desires which are determined by man's power or reason, are always good; the others may be good as well as evil.*

*There is no rational life, therefore, without intelligence and things are good only insofar as they assist man to enjoy that life of the mind which is determined by intelligence. Those things alone, on the other hand, we call evil which hinder man from perfecting his reason and enjoying a rational life. But because all those things of which man is the efficient cause are necessarily good, it follows that no evil can happen to man except from external causes, that is to say, except insofar as he is a part of the whole Nature, whose laws human nature is compelled to obey—compelled also to accommodate himself to this whole of Nature in almost an infinite number of ways.*

*Anything that exists in Nature which we judge to be evil or able to hinder us from existing and enjoying a rational life, we are allowed to remove from us in that way which seems the safest; and whatever, on the other hand, we judge to be good or to be profitable for the preservation of our being or the enjoyment of a rational life, we are permitted to take for our use and use in any way we may think proper; and absolutely, everyone is allowed by the highest right of Nature to do that which he believes contributes to his own profit.*

*Insofar as men are carried away by envy or any emotion of hatred towards one another, so far are they contrary to one another, and consequently so much the more are they to be feared, as they have more power than other individuals of nature.*

*Minds, nevertheless, are not conquered by arms, but by love and generosity. Above all things is it profitable to men to form communities and to unite themselves to one another by bonds which may make all of them as one man; and absolutely, it is profitable for them to do whatever may tend to strengthen their friendships.*

*Although, therefore, men generally determine everything by their pleasure, many more advantages than disadvantages arise from their common union. It is better, therefore, to endure with equanimity the injuries inflicted by them, and to apply our minds to those things which subserve concord and the establishment of friendship.*

*Concord, moreover, is often produced by fear, but it is without good faith. It is to be observed, too, that fear arises from impotence of mind and therefore is of no service to reason; nor is pity, although it seems to present an appearance of piety.*

*In the receipt of benefits and in returning thanks, care altogether different must be taken.*

*The love of a harlot, that is to say, the lust of sexual intercourse, which arises from mere external form, and absolutely all love which recognizes any other cause than the freedom of the mind, easily passes into hatred, unless, which is worse, it becomes a species of delirium, and thereby discord is cherished rather than concord.*

*Flattery, too, produces concord, but only by means of the disgraceful crime of slavery or perfidy; for there are none who are more taken by flattery than the proud, who wish to be first and are not so.*

*There is a false appearance of piety and religion in dejection; and although dejection is the opposite of pride, the humble dejected man is very near akin to the proud.*

*Shame also contributes to concord, but only with regard to those matters which cannot be concealed. Shame, too, inasmuch as it is a kind of sorrow, does not belong to the service of reason.*

*Superstition, on the contrary, seems to affirm that what brings sorrow is good, and on the contrary, that what brings joy is evil. But, as we have already said, no one, excepting an envious man, is delighted at my impotence or disadvantage, for the greater the joy with which we are affected, the greater the perfection to which we pass, and consequently the more do we participate in the divine nature; nor can joy ever be evil which is controlled by a true consideration for our own profit. On the other hand, the man who is led by fear, and does what is good that he may avoid what is evil, is not guided by reason.*

*The man who has properly understood that everything follows from the necessity of the divine nature, and comes to pass according to the eternal laws and rules of Nature, will in truth discover nothing which is worthy of hatred, laughter, or contempt, nor will he pity anyone, but, so far as human virtue is able, he will endeavor to do well, as we say, and to rejoice.*

*God is the efficient cause not only of the existence of things, but also of their essence.*

*Individual things are nothing but modifications of the attributes of God, or modes by which the attributes of God are expressed in a fixed and definite manner.*

CHAPTER TEN

# John Locke

**(1632–1704)**

- **There are no innate ideas**
- **Freedom is the ability to "choose"**
- **Our God-given rights are: life, liberty, and property**

Locke can be understood as an easygoing Hobbes. His influence on philosophy and government are simply immeasurable. In the American Declaration of Independence and in the Constitution you'll find more "Lockian" concepts than you can count.

John Locke was the son of an attorney in Bristol, England. Pushed by his father to become a minister, Locke rejected this occupation and went on to study both philosophy and medicine. Like all the smart English guys in this book, Locke eventually finished his studies at Oxford. While there, Locke was extremely influenced by the idea of religious tolerance; he wanted to find a common ground between conflicting religious sects. These democratic views were considered a challenge to the monarchy in general, but particularly to the authority of James II, so Locke fled to Holland in 1682. After the Civil War and the subsequent exile of James II, he returned to England in 1689. By the time he died fifteen years later at Oates, he was a famous philosopher, political thinker, and revolutionary figure.

## Locke's Big Idea #1: The Blank Slate

John Locke argued that each one of us is born a "Tabula Rasa." For the few of you who don't speak fluent Latin, that translates as "blank slate." Each one of us began with a blank slate, that is, with no innate ethical or moral principles. (What would Plato think?)

Therefore, he believes that all knowledge is derived from experience—the empiricist theory.

In other words, if morality is not innate, then our moral notions must be based on experience, self-preservation, and the pursuit of happiness. Our senses drive our ideas and our human knowledge is limited to those things that have some basis in sensation or experience. This epistemological (theory of knowledge) conception goes against Descartes' and Spinoza's view that humans have innate principles and ideas that can be unquestionably demonstrated. For Locke, we can never have absolute knowledge of anything like the essence or form of "real" substance in the world.

However, our ideas about the external world with its shapes, extensions, and motions do closely represent the external bodies themselves. Note that Locke takes the "reality" of the external world as a given, stating that some of our ideas closely represent these eternal phenomena. We can therefore have an adequate understanding of the causes at work in nature.

While we can never directly apprehend the nature of substance, Locke contends that there must be some substratum which causes these representative ideas. He says the essential nature substance, is "a something I know not what."

**Bessie the Unicorn**

Even my idea of Bessie the Cow with a unicorn horn stuck to her head is derived from experience. While I have never seen a cow with a horn on its head (nor have I ever seen Bessie—although I've become quite fond of the idea of her), this imaginative concept of a cow-unicorn is simply a result of the mind's capacity to relate one idea from experience (a horn) and another idea of experience (a cow).

While we can never come to an absolute knowledge of the metaphysical reality of things such as "substance" or "form" or "essences," in the end we know enough to secure our "great concernments." That is to say, we know enough to know how to live a better life and how to behave. But it must be said that the certainty of Descartes' and Spinoza's method of enquiry, based on conceptions like "substance," "essence" and the like, are seriously called into question by Locke.

## Locke's Big Idea #2: Natural Rights

Like Hobbes, Locke believes that out of a "state of nature" (before government), humankind enters into a social contract with some sovereign power for protection. However, Locke asserts that the state of nature was not a violent and horrible place due to mankind's selfish and brutish instincts. On the contrary, Locke sees man's natural state as one of relative kindness and cooperation. Human beings entered into a social contract and formed governments because it provided greater stability and protection, not because life was so awful and violent. Locke's understanding of the state of nature and the natural instincts of man provides him with the idea that man has certain "natural rights." These natural rights are God-given: life, liberty, and property (remember the Declaration of Independence!!). Locke's view that property is a "natural right" is one of his more famous claims. According to him, in the "State of Nature," humans did have an understanding of property. However, to protect this God-given right, people formed governments.

## Locke's Big Idea #3: People Should Rule Themselves

Locke believes that since there are natural rights God gave man, the government should uphold them. If government infringes upon even one of those rights, it has abused its power. A government like this should be overthrown. For Hobbes, the only reason for revolt is when the government loses its power and control. For Locke, government power should be restricted from infringing upon "natural rights." If it does abuse its power, get rid of it! The importance of limiting the abuse of power led Locke to advocate some kind of representative government. The role of the legislature is extremely important for Locke. These concepts form the foundation of some of our most cherished political ideals. Now there's a guy who makes sense!

*We are utterly incapable of universal and certain Knowledge.*

*What worries you, masters you.*

*Wherever Law ends, Tyranny begins.*

*There is frequently more to be learned from the unexpected questions of a child than the discourses of men.*

*Reverie is when ideas float in our mind without reflection or regard of the understanding.*

*Reading furnishes the mind only with material for knowledge; it is thinking that makes what we read ours.*

*Parents wonder why the streams are bitter, when they themselves have poisoned the fountain.*

*If we will disbelieve everything, because we cannot certainly know all things, we shall do much what as wisely as he who would not use his legs, but sit still and perish, because he had no wings to fly.*

*The dread of evil is a much more forcible principle of human actions than the prospect of good.*

*The actions of men are the best interpreters of their thoughts.*

*No man's knowledge here can go beyond his experience.*

*To understand political power aright, and derive it from its original, we must consider what estate all men are naturally in, and that is, a state of perfect freedom.*

*And reason . . . teaches all mankind who will but consult it, that being all equal and independent, no one ought to harm another in his life, health, liberty or possessions.*

*Every man has a property in his own person. This nobody has a right to, but himself.*

*Government has no other end than the preservation of property.*

*A ruling body that offends against the natural law must be deposed.*

*Good and evil, reward and punishment, are the only motives to a rational creature: These are the spur and reins whereby all mankind are set on work, and guided.*

CHAPTER ELEVEN

# David Hume

**(1711–1776)**

- Took Lockian empiricism to a point of skepticism
- Denied the rational basis for Cause and Effect
- Denied the rational basis for the external world

The image I have of David Hume is that of an older, British gentleman who one day (while reading Spinoza probably) stood up and yelled "enough metaphysical nonsense!" While it is not a matter of historical fact that he did so, one can infer from his work a desire to once and for all discover the limits of human knowledge, and keep philosophy from seeking unattainable truths.

Born in Edinburgh, Scotland, David Hume went on to graduate from Edinburgh University with a degree in law. He became a politician, holding a few public offices. Then he dedicated himself to philosophy, hoping to have the same effect in this field as Newton did in science. Okay, so he wasn't the most modest of men. His first writings received little acclaim, and he was forced to support himself as a librarian, diplomat, and essayist. While his historical writings on England finally offered him a modest living as a writer, the firm establishment of his reputation as an essential philosopher did not come about until after his death.

Nonetheless, Hume is a pivotal figure in philosophy. He tried to rid philosophy of all spiritual enquiry. The soul, the universe, and even the "self"—all are absolutely without rational justification, according to Hume. Spinoza took the Scholastic and Cartesian conceptions of the nature of "substance" and "God" to their logical conclusions, and Hume did the same with the empirical perspectives of Locke and Hobbes.

## Hume's Big Idea #1: We Really Don't Know Anything

Hume's contention: Knowledge is supposedly derived from experience of the external world, but there is no rational proof that such an external world exists at all. According to Hume, our "idea" of something is merely a copy of our immediate "impression." Colors and sounds, pleasure and pain are examples of "impressions." Our "ideas" are just faint imitations of these impressions. Since we can never know what, if anything, caused these impressions and sensations, we can never provide a rational determination of an external world. In other words, we really don't necessarily know anything.

### Bessie Is Bessie the Cow

Locke claimed that our knowledge of Bessie the Cow is based on the necessary fact that something has caused our perception of her, namely her. The Bessie we see is some kind of mediated representation of a real existent object. Hume goes further and says that we can provide no rational basis that our idea of her is a representation of anything.

Furthermore, Hume says that even if there is an external world, all conceptions of "cause" and "effect" relationships in scientific study are impossible to determine rationally. For example, if I let go of Bessie from the top of the Empire State Building and after she leaves my hand she falls to the ground, what am I really witnessing? The scientific claim of his day is that my letting go of her is the "cause" of her fall. *But we can never know the nature of Bessie* other than our mediated experience of her (assuming Bessie exists at all). Therefore, we can only come to the conclusion that one event, letting go of her, has preceded the second event, her splattering on 34th Street. The idea that my letting go of Bessie "produced" or "caused" her fall is not rationally demonstrable. This conception of "cause" is just an assumption that we make out of the habit of witnessing one event that is preceded by another. But there is no rational basis for concluding that this will always be the case, for we cannot conclude that something actually "caused" something else. We can therefore only assume that what happened in the past will happen in the future. Although cause and effect and the external world have no rational justification and occur out of our assumptions and habits, as Hume famously admits, "It still would not be wise for me to throw myself out of the window." While we can provide no rational basis that it will turn out badly for Hume if he does so, it's just better to be safe than sorry.

What do we make of this skepticism? Is the truth of any belief rationally demonstrable? For Hume, only what he calls "relations of ideas" are demonstrable. That is, the mathematical fact that a square has four sides is demonstrably true because it requires absolutely no reference to an external world that we cannot TRULY KNOW, a world that for all rational purposes might not even be there at all.

## Hume's Big Idea #2: Moral Properties Derived from Sense

According to Hume, there are no absolute moral properties or laws with objective reality. That is to say, morals are not "in the world." This is opposite Plato's view, where the idea or form of something like "Justice" has an independent and objective reality outside our apprehension of it. For Hume, on the other hand, morals are completely subjective feelings and sensations that human beings are disposed to have.

For example, take the Grand Canyon. Is this work of nature really beautiful? Plato would say that "Beauty" is a "real" thing in the world and the "beauty" of the Grand Canyon is a fact, actually contained within the Grand Canyon. Hume, an empiricist, like Locke and Hobbes before him, claims that "beauty" is not a "real" thing in the world but just a subjective reaction that human beings have when they look at the Grand Canyon. The same logic applies to his view of morality. As Hume famously says, "look at the willful murder in all its facts and relations and the viciousness completely escapes you." In other words, the "viciousness" of murder, just like the "beauty" of the Grand Canyon, is just a subjective response particular to and only "real" in the sensations of human beings.

Just as I let go of Bessie, Hume let go of all the philosophical claims before him. Both Locke's claim that the external world causes sensation, as well as the metaphysical claims that God caused the world, are thrown out the window by Hume's skeptical hands. His skepticism raised important points and questions that had to be addressed . . . by . . . Oh, thank God! Kant to the rescue!

*Where ambition can cover its enterprises, even to the person himself, under the appearance of principle, it is the most incurable and inflexible of passions.*

*It is seldom that liberty of any kind is lost all at once.*

*Art may make a suit of clothes: but nature must produce a man.*

*Beauty in things exists in the mind which contemplates them.*

*Custom is the great guide of human life.*

*The heights of popularity and patriotism are still the beaten road to power and tyranny; flattery to treachery; standing armies to arbitrary government; and the glory of God to the temporal interest of the clergy.*

*It is not reason which is the guide of life, but custom.*

*Habit may lead us to belief and expectation but not to the knowledge, and still less to the understanding, of lawful relations.*

*If we take in our hand any volume; of divinity or school metaphysics, for instance; let us ask, "Does it contain any abstract reasoning concerning quantity or number?" No. "Does it contain any experimental reasoning concerning matter of fact and existence?" No. Commit it then to the flames: For it can contain nothing but sophistry and illusion.*

*The great end of all human industry is the attainment of happiness. For this were arts invented, sciences cultivated, laws ordained, and societies modeled, by the most profound wisdom of patriots and legislators. Even the lonely savage, who lies exposed to the inclemency of the elements and the fury of wild beasts, forgets not, for a moment, this grand object of his being.*

*A wise man proportions his belief to the evidence.*

*The heart of man is made to reconcile contradiction.*

*In all determinations of morality, this circumstance of public utility is ever principally in view; wherever disputes arise, either in philosophy or common life, concerning the bounds of duty, the question cannot, by any means, be decided with greater certainty, that by ascertaining . . . the true interests of mankind.*

*Truth springs from argument amongst friends.*

*Learning has been [a] great loser by being shut up in colleges and cells and secluded from the world and good company.*

*Extinguish all warm feelings and prepossessions in favor of virtue, and all disgust and aversion to vice: Render men totally indifferent towards these distinctions; and morality is no longer a practical study, nor has any tendency to regulate our lives and actions.*

*Can anything stronger be said of a profession . . . than to observe the advantages which it procures to society? And is not the monk and the inquisitor enraged when we treat his order as useless and pernicious to mankind?*

*Giving alms to a beggar is naturally praised because it seems to carry relief to the distressed and indigent: But when we observe the encouragement thence arising to idleness and debauchery, we regard this species of charity rather as a weakness than a virtue.*

CHAPTER TWELVE

# Immanuel Kant

**(1724–1804)**

- The most influential modern philosopher
- Provided an entirely new foundation for human knowledge
- Asserted an entirely new foundation for moral action

Immanuel Kant is the most influential philosopher of modern times. He revolutionized the philosophical world with his "Critique of Pure Reason," much like the Beatles revolutionized the world of music with Sgt. Pepper's.

At first glance, Kant seems an unlikely candidate for a philosopher. He was born to simple, lower-class folk in Königsberg, Germany. After receiving a pious Lutheran education, at sixteen he was admitted to the University of Königsberg, where he eventually held a professorship. Unlike most philosophers we have studied, Kant did not travel. In fact, he never left the vicinity of his hometown, ever! Kant began his philosophical writings in his late fifties. For the most part, his personal life was stable, perhaps even a little dull. He spent his philosophical years writing by his window, inspired by his view of a cathedral. Every morning, he woke up at the same hour. His daily walks occurred with such regularity that it was said that you could set your clock to his approach. But while he may not have been the most exciting chap, he is certainly a revolutionary philosophical figure.

## Kant's Big Idea: Space and Time

According to Kant, two obvious structures of our experience precede our sensations. These are the concepts of space and time. To wit: The mind orders all our sense data into both space and time. These structures precede and determine experience itself. Kant claimed that causation and substance are also structures of the mind that precede experience. Our experience is necessarily ordered by the universal structures of space and time.

## Bessie the Cow

For instance, Kant would say (like Hume), we can never know the nature of Bessie the Cow outside of our experience of her. But on the other hand, if Bessie is painted yellow and then blue, we recognize more than just a change in color (i.e., sensation). In fact, we recognize that the same entity (the cow) has undergone change. By the fact that our experience occurs in time, we can understand the succession of events from a blue cow to a yellow cow, indicating a "cause" of that change. While the empiricists, such as Locke or Hume, would claim universal knowledge about our world is impossible, Kant says we can have universal ("A priori" or "Not based on experience") knowledge of certain principles, such as the laws of nature.

Even though we are limited to knowing that which is within our experience (we can't talk about God or substances like Spinoza does) we can still have knowledge of a world that is not derived from experience. To make this clear, Locke, Hume, Hobbes, and all other empiricists make two claims about knowledge. The first is that humans are limited to knowledge of their experience. That is to say, unlike Plato or Aristotle, we can never understand the true nature of a table or chair beyond our experience of that table. This seems rather intuitive.

But the second claim (the one Kant opposes) is that knowledge is therefore derived from experience. This is a mistake, according to Kant, because it is the case that our experience has necessary and universal structures. Our mind gives itself these structures so that our experience can be ordered and intelligible. So if our experience is ordered by structures such as space and time, these structures must precede and determine experience. Thus, through the use of reason we can have a priori or "experience-free" knowledge with regard to those things which are within or pertain to our experience.

The laws of nature, for example, are therefore an object of knowledge and are rationally demonstrable. Because, according to Kant, they do not explain the way the world actually is, but instead are merely universal principles of the way in which we experience that world.

It is important to note that Kant conceives of the human mind, like the ancients did, as having an active role. We are not just Lockian blank slates deriving our knowledge from experience, but we ourselves—our minds—set the conditions and the structures for the way in which this experience will occur.

For Kant, to be moral one must "Act so that your maxim can be willed as a universal law." This is Kant's "categorical imperative." Let's see how it works.

To expose the contradictory character of immoral or amoral maxims, Kant examines the maxim "promises should always be broken." For Kant, the "categorical imperative" will show that this is a logical contradiction, and necessarily non-moral in character.

The reason that this maxim cannot be a universal moral command is that the word "promise" would be starved of all meaning. Furthermore, to hold a conception of "promises" and therefore "promise-keeping" (for within the concept of promise is the understanding that it should be kept), and to also hold that "all promises should be broken," is a logical contradiction. It's basically the same as saying, "We will have these agreements called promises and we will always break them." So, why even have such a word at all? The categorical imperative is a kind of logical "test" that is supposed to expose and seperate that which is a moral command and that must be followed, from that which is either amoral or immoral in character.

Kant's epistemological and moral theories are as fascinating as they are tricky. We can know our experience because it is necessarily ordered in space and time. Pretty heady stuff for a small-town boy of modest upbringing who never even bothered to leave home.

*Although all knowledge begins from experience it does not necessarily spring from experience.*

*Have patience awhile; slanders are not long-lived. Truth is the child of time; erelong she shall appear to vindicate thee.*

*Science is organized knowledge. Wisdom is organized life.*

*The history of the human race, viewed as a whole, may be regarded as the realization of a hidden plan of nature to bring about a political constitution, internally, and for this purpose, also externally perfect, as the only state in which all the capacities implanted by her in mankind can be fully developed.*

*It is not necessary that whilst I live I live happily; but it is necessary that so long as I live I should live honorably.*

*The human heart refuses to believe in a universe without purpose.*

*The bad thing of war is, that it makes more evil people than it can take away.*

*The function of the true state is to impose the minimum restrictions and safeguard the maximum liberties of the people, and it never regards the person as a thing.*

*The eternal mystery of the world is its comprehensibility.*

*Always recognize that human individuals are ends, and do not use them as means to your end.*

*Experience without theory is blind, but theory without experience is mere intellectual play.*

*To be is to do.*

*Happiness is not an ideal of reason, but of imagination.*

*Science is organized knowledge. Wisdom is organized life.*

*Metaphysics is a dark ocean without shores or lighthouse, strewn with many a philosophic wreck.*

*In law a man is guilty when he violates the rights of others. In ethics he is guilty if he only thinks of doing so.*

*Intuition and concepts constitute the elements of all our knowledge, so that neither concepts without an intuition in some way corresponding to them, nor intuition without concepts, can yield knowledge.*

*Two things fill the mind with ever new and increasing wonder and awe— the starry heavens above me and the moral law within me.*

*Only the descent into the hell of self-knowledge prepares the way for godliness.*

*For when moral value is considered, the concern is not the actions, which are seen, but rather with their inner principles, which are not seen.*

*It is not God's will merely that we should be happy, but that we should make ourselves happy.*

CHAPTER THIRTEEN

# G.W.F. Hegel

**(1770–1831)**

- **History as progression of freedom**
- **Philosophy of Absolute Idealism**
- **Reality is Rational**

Hegel is unquestionably the most ambitious and systematic thinker since Aristotle. His ideas captivated German intellectual society the way Bruce Springsteen captivates the New Jersey working man.

Born in Stuttgart, Germany, Hegel had a picture-perfect upbringing in a close and loving family. His mother was a homemaker and his father was a minor government official. Hegel eventually studied at Tübingen University, where, due to his less than enthusiastic attitude to his work, his diploma read that he had a fair understanding of theology, and an inadequate understanding of philosophy. But Hegel showed them! He worked as a private tutor and high school teacher, before eventually securing a chair of philosophy at the University of Berlin. He received notable recognition there, and in the last ten years of his life became famous throughout Europe.

Like all philosophers of his day, Hegel admired Kant and accepted his basic ideas. But if you remember, while Kant secured our knowledge of universal truths of the world of our experience, he still left the world beyond our experience unknowable. Hegel was unsatisfied with this.

## Hegel's Big Idea #1: The World Makes Sense

According to Hegel, the natural world is rational. What, you say? The world itself is rational? Yes, Hegel asserts. The physical world is rational and imbued with meaning. Everything on earth is a manifestation of the world spirit or *Weltgeist*, whose realization in the world is a rational, dialectical process. The ultimate reality is the Idea or Mind (that which knows). Hegel's Absolute Idealism contends that everything that exists is absolutely and essentially related to an Absolute Idea, Mind, or Spirit.

All right, we'll back up. Let's start with Hegel's dialectic. His dialectic is the logical process for how truth is discovered. The process is thesis, antithesis and synthesis. The synthesis is the higher form of truth. It is the unity of the opposites of thesis and antithesis.

**Hegelian Dialectic**
Thesis: Concept of "Being"
Antithesis: Concept of "Nothing"
Synthesis: Concept of "Becoming"

Basically, from the concept of "Being," one thinks of the opposite concept of "Nothing." But knowledge doesn't end there. The "higher truth" in the development of knowledge comes by way of the synthesis of two opposite concepts. Hence, "Being" and "Nothing" are synthesized to create the new concept of "Becoming."

We find this dialectic not just in our human consciousness, helping us to understand the world, but also in the world itself. The world itself is a process in which the ultimate reality (Spirit) unfolds itself into actual (physical) entities. Thus we can understand everything in the world, because everything is a result of the Absolute Spirit (or Mind).

## Hegel's Big Idea #2: History Has a Purpose

Famous for his view of history, Hegel traces the development of the world spirit in terms of a quest for freedom. History is the progressive development of that freedom. History has a purpose. That purpose is rational: It is the unfolding of the idea of freedom in human consciousness.

The first stage of freedom is the recognition of the self as opposed to its antithesis, "the other." Think of a master and slave. While the slave is dominated by the master, he nevertheless labors and creates. His identity is established with regard to his labor or cre-ation. Meanwhile, the master is dependent on both the slave's labor, as well as his recognition as "Master." By dominating the slave, the master is also dominated by his dependence. Ultimately, then, neither the slave nor the master is free. This realization is the synthesis of the thesis and antithesis.

Once this realization is accepted, human history can go on to a new level of mentality. Human history, therefore, is a process in which the Absolute Spirit manifests itself in human consciousness through the synthesis of thesis and antithesis, refining the Idea of Freedom as it goes.

Hegel contends that the final embodiment of the Spirit is found in the modern Constitutional State. The State itself will determine morality and ethical conduct; for Hegel, it is only within the social context of the State that the individual can be free. Individual freedom for Hegel has true value and meaning only in this context.

In the decade after Hegel's death, many Germans considered themselves "Hegelians." While this did not last forever, his impact on philosophers such as Karl Marx, as well as many others, can't be denied. Not to mention that Hegel's uniquely systematic and ambitious philosophical undertaking is inspirational.

*What is real is rational; what is rational is real.*

*What experience and history teach is this—that people and governments never have learned anything from history, or acted on principles deduced from it.*

*Genuine tragedies in the world are not conflicts between right and wrong. They are conflicts between two rights.*

*Governments have never learned anything from history, or acted on principles deducted from it.*

*I'm not ugly, but my beauty is a total creation.*

*Mark this well, you proud men of action! You are, after all, nothing but unconscious instruments of the men of thought.*

*Nothing great in the world has ever been accomplished without passion.*

*Only one man ever understood me, and he didn't understand me.*

*Too fair to worship, too divine to love.*

*The only Thought, which Philosophy brings . . . to the contemplation of History, is the simple conception of Reason; that Reason is the Sovereign of the world, that the history of the world, therefore, presents us with a rational process.*

*Spirit is self-contained existence. Now this is Freedom, exactly. For if I am dependent, my being is referred to something which I am not; I cannot exist independently of something external. I am free, on the contrary, when my existence depends on myself.*

*The History of the world is none other than the progress of the consciousness of Freedom . . . The destiny of the spiritual world, and the final cause of the World at large, we claim to be Spirit's consciousness of its own freedom, and ipso facto, the reality of that freedom . . . This final aim is God's purpose with the world; but God is the absolutely perfect Being, and can, therefore, will nothing but himself.*

*All the worth which the human being possesses, all spiritual reality, he possesses only through the State . . . For Truth is the unity of the universal and subjective will; and the Universal is to be found in the State, in its laws, its universal and rational arrangements. The State is the Divine Idea as it exists on earth. We have in it, therefore, the object of history in a more definite shape than before; that in which Freedom obtains objectivity. For Law is the objectivity of the Spirit.*

*The nation lives the same kind of life as the individual . . . in the enjoyment of itself, the satisfaction of being exactly what it desired to be . . . [and the consequent] abandonment of aspirations . . . [the nation slips into a] merely customary life (like the watch wound up and going on of itself), into an activity without opposition. And this is what brings on its natural death . . . Thus perish individuals, and thus perish nations, by a natural death.*

*What experience and history teach is this—that people and governments never have learned anything from history, or acted on principles deduced from it.*

*The significance of that 'absolute commandment,' know thyself—whether we look at it in itself or under the historical circumstances of its first utterance—is not to promote mere self-knowledge in respect of the particular capacities, character, propensities, and foibles of the single self. The knowledge it commands means that of man's genuine reality—of what is essentially and ultimately true and real—of spirit as the true and essential being.*

*Each of the parts of philosophy is a philosophical whole, a circle rounded and complete in itself. In each of these parts, however, the philosophical Idea is found in a particular specificity or medium. The single circle, because it is a real totality, bursts through the limits imposed by its special medium, and gives rise to a wider circle. The whole of philosophy in this way resembles a circle of circles. The Idea appears in each single circle, but, at the same time, the whole Idea is constituted by the system of these peculiar phases, and each is a necessary member of the organization.*

*The first glance at History convinces us that the actions of men proceed from their needs, their passions, their characters and talents; and impresses us with the belief that such needs, passions, and interests are the sole spring of actions.*

*It is easier to discover a deficiency in individuals, in states, and in Providence, than to see their real import and value.*

*Mere goodness can achieve little against the power of nature.*

*The courage of the truth is the first condition of philosophic study.*

CHAPTER FOURTEEN

# Karl Marx

**(1818–1883)**

- Philosopher of action
- Revolutionized our way of thinking about society
- History as "class conflict"

Karl Marx is the philosopher with a mission. When we think of Karl Marx, we think of revolution, power, and human suffering. The image of an academic elitist, droning on about irrelevant things, does not come to mind when we think of Marx. We think of a man whose philosophy has been put into action, and whose relevance continues until this day.

Marx came into this world the third in a family of nine children in Trier, Germany. His parents were of Jewish ancestry, but they had converted to Protestantism to protect his father's job as a government lawyer. Marx, the atypical philosopher, was not a model student. He spent most of his time drinking while at the University of Bonn. He cleaned up his act and began to focus on his studies, eventually achieving a doctorate in philosophy from the University of Jena.

His leftist politics made it difficult for him to obtain a professorship. He moved to Cologne, where he became a very successful newspaper editor; he went on from there to Paris, where he hung out with the other socialists of his day. It was there that he met his lifelong friend, collaborator, and financial backer, Frederick Engels. Marx eventually settled in London, where he struggled to make a living due to his poor money management. Later in life, while he was more secure financially, he suffered nonetheless from boils all over his body, treating them with arsenic and opium to no avail. He died of bronchitis in 1883.

## Marx's Big Idea: We Are Living in a Material World

Like Hegel, Marx thought history to be a dialectical process. However, according to Marx, this process was not guided by an Absolute Spirit, but rather by the economic forces and class struggles of mankind. Marx is a materialist—just as Aristotle brought Platonic forms down from the sky and put them into the things themselves, Marx takes Hegel's historical dialectic and brings it down to the material world.

Marx contends that out of the conflict between the upper class and the lower class arose a new economic system and a new class: *The Bourgeoisie*. Capitalist owners exploit and alienate the proletariat (working class), thus provoking what Marx considers the final class conflict.

The alienation of workers in the Industrial period was due to the nature of the labor itself, according to Marx. Workers had no attachment to their product (as opposed to farmers and peasants, who had a connection to the land they worked). In addition, the interests of one class always contradict the interests of another. This intensification of the dialectic, according to Marx, was an indication that it was the final struggle.

Marx is often misunderstood as the political thinker who came up with Communism as "the ideal society." It's true that Marx believed that Communism, a classless society without private property, would be a better society. But his claim was stronger than that. Marx claimed that it is historically inevitable that Capitalism will destroy itself and the Proletariat will rise. Furthermore, in his dialectal view, every period of history was necessary and inevitable, even the Capitalist system which he loathed.

Capitalism provided the means and the method for increasing the quantity of production. It was a necessary stage, because its complete opposite, Communism, would then arise, and this wealth and productive capability could be equally distributed and publicly owned. Marx says that the Communist State will be the opposite of the Capitalist one, an opposite that he thinks will be the final epoch of the historical dialectic, a final epoch that will benefit all humankind.

Oops, well, we all make mistakes. Of course, over a century after Marx first published his work, Capitalism is alive and well and Communism lives on in only a few states.

But seriously, though, Marx gets a bad rap. The most important contribution Marx makes to philosophic thought is that, while other philosophers and historians had hitherto looked at the philosophy, religion, and literature of the past to understand society, Marx considered the foundation of social organization to be the economic forces of exchange, distribution, and consumption. The legacy of his thought is everywhere today, as many modern thinkers look to these forces to explain the past, the present, as well as the alternative economic structures that may better our lives.

*The philosophers have only interpreted the world, in various ways; the point, however, is to change it.*

*The writer must earn money in order to be able to live and to write, but he must by no means live and write for the purpose of making money.*

*The ruling ideas of each age have ever been the ideas of its ruling class.*

*Sell a man a fish, he eats for a day, teach a man how to fish, you ruin a wonderful business opportunity.*

*From each according to his abilities, to each according to his needs.*

*The rich will do anything for the poor but get off their backs.*

*Reason has always existed, but not always in a reasonable form.*

*Philosophy is to the real world as masturbation is to sex.*

*The tradition of all the dead generations weighs like a nightmare on the brain of the living.*

*Man will often act and live as though he were apart from his body, as if improving it from the outside.*

*The meaning of peace is the absence of opposition to Socialism.*

*My object in life is to dethrone God and destroy capitalism.*

*History does nothing; it does not possess immense riches, it does not fight battles. It is men, real, living, who do all this.*

*Capital is money, capital is commodities. By virtue of it being value, it has acquired the occult ability to add value to itself. It brings forth living off-spring, or, at the least, lays golden eggs.*

*Experience praises the most happy the one who made the most people happy.*

*On a level plain, simple mounds look like hills; and the insipid flatness of our present bourgeoisie is to be measured by the altitude of its "great intellects."*

*The workers have nothing but their chains to lose in this. They have a world to win.*

*Workers of the world, unite!*

*History repeats. First as tragedy, then as farce.*

*Who will teach the teachers?*

*The policy of Russia is changeless. Its methods, its tactics, its maneuvers may change, but the polar star of its policy, world domination, is a fixed star.*

*The only antidote to mental suffering is physical pain.*

*Mankind always sets itself only such tasks as it can solve; since, looking at the matter more closely, we will always find that the task itself arises only when the material conditions necessary for its solution already exist or are at least in the process of formation.*

*Landlords, like all other men, love to reap where they never sowed.*

*The writer may very well serve a movement of history as its mouthpiece, but he cannot of course create it.*

*Anyone who knows anything of history knows that great social changes are impossible without feminine upheaval. Social progress can be measured exactly by the social position of the fair sex, the ugly ones included.*

*Religion . . . is the opium of the masses.*

*If Karl, instead of writing a lot about capital, had made a lot of it, it would have been much better.*

—Karl Marx's mother

*Go on, get out. Last words are for fools who haven't said enough.*

—Marx saying goodbye to his housekeeper

CHAPTER FIFTEEN

# Jean-Jacques Rousseau

**(1712-1788)**

- Asserted the idea of "general will"
- An important figure in democratic thought
- Ideas fueled French Revolution

Jean-Jacques Rousseau's influence on the real world was as great as his influence on philosophy. His writings served as a kind of textbook for the French Revolution.

Rousseau was born in Geneva, Switzerland, in 1712. His mother died during his birth. His father was a violent and dissipated man who did not give the young Rousseau a lick of intellectual training. Finally, he deserted the boy altogether and Rousseau was sent to become an apprentice, both as a coppersmith and as a notary. The strict discipline drove him to run away in 1728. After that, Rousseau's life was one of constant change and turmoil. He embraced Catholicism and then Protestantism.

Over time, Rousseau developed a love of both philosophy and music. Eventually, when he was more than forty years old, he became recognized in Paris as a prize-winning author and even wrote a successful operetta. Known for his brilliant work, as well as his vanity and his recklessness, Rousseau never failed to receive attention from then on. His controversial stance on freedom of religion and his opposition to the Church, as well as his propensity for obsessive relationships and a deep paranoia of his friends, caused Rousseau to relocate all around Europe.

One of his last works was burned by the French parliament and an order for his arrest forced him to relocate once again, this time to the Swiss city of Berne (occupied by Prussia at the time). Here, after advocating for freedom of religion from the Church and the police, local peasants and the government of Berne drove him out. David Hume, the noted philosopher, offered him asylum in England, where he stayed until, once again, his morbid misanthropy and paranoia led him to quarrels with his friends, and he fled back to France. After being permitted back in Paris in 1770, he wrote and studied music until he accepted an invitation to retire in Ermenonville, where he died suddenly.

## Rousseau's Big Idea #1: The Social Contract

Like John Locke, Rousseau's conception of the "State of Nature" was one of general pleasantness. Rousseau's writings stress the idea that human beings were in a "perfect state of freedom" during the pre-social era. However, humans joined together to form governments, compromising their individual freedom to meet the needs of the community. Like Locke, Rousseau believes private property is one of the driving forces behind this "social contract." Rousseau claims that government's role should be the execution of the general **will**.

## Rousseau's Big Idea #2: The General Will

Rousseau contends that slavery or military conquest does not provide a legitimate rule. Rousseau's social contract asserts that every individual voluntarily participates in the social contract. This leads Rousseau to what he takes to be an indestructible principle, the general will.

The general will is the "will of all." Not just the sum of different individual wills, but a will that everyone shares for the benefit of all. Society is best organized when each individual participates in this general will.

### Bessie and the Other Cows

All the cows in Bessie the Cow's society share a common "will," a common national or collective consciousness. For the benefit of all the cows in this society, Bessie must give up her individual desire to vote against the "grass ration" bill, a bill which states, due to the lack of adequate rainfall, that each cow can only have a pound a day of grass. Bessie is big and can push all the other cows away, eating as much as she wants. But she is a part of the general will and she knows that the law will benefit the society. She must relinquish her individual desires and wholly participate in the general will.

By entering into the social contract, it is incumbent upon the individual to surrender his interests for the good of society, regardless of the personal consequences of that surrender. The **general will** must be concerned solely with the **general interest** of society.

For this reason, Rousseau does not necessarily insist on democracy. Any government that executes the general will works for him. While Rousseau encourages public discussion and debate, he worries that special interests will compromise the general will (don't we all share that fear!).

He believes that the general will is an indestructible principle of society. According to Rousseau, each nation has a different general will, dependent upon a number of factors, even weather and climate.

*An honest man nearly always thinks justly.*

*The person who is slowest in making a promise is most faithful in its performance.*

*The training of children is a profession, where we must know how to waste time in order to save it.*

*Falsehood has an infinity of combinations, but truth has only one mode of being.*

*Virtue is a state of war, and to live in it we have always to combat with ourselves.*

*At sixteen, the adolescent knows about suffering because he himself has suffered, but he barely knows that other beings also suffer.*

*Man is born free and everywhere he is in chains.*

*Good laws lead to the making of better ones; bad ones bring about worse.*

*A feeble body weakens the mind.*

*Whoever blushes is already guilty; true innocence is ashamed of nothing.*

*Every man has a right to risk his own life for the preservation of it.*

*General and abstract ideas are the source of the greatest errors of mankind.*

*Happiness: a good bank account, a good cook, and a good digestion.*

*How many famous and high-spirited heroes have lived a day too long?*

*Nature never deceives us; it is we who deceive ourselves.*

*People who know little are usually great talkers, while men who know much say little.*

*The person who has lived the most is not the one with the most years, but the one with the richest experiences.*

*We are born weak, we need strength; helpless, we need aid; foolish, we need reason. All that we lack at birth, all that we need when we come to man's estate, is the gift of education.*

*What wisdom can you find that is greater than kindness?*

*A country cannot subsist well without liberty, nor liberty without virtue.*

*Watch a cat when it enters a room for the first time. It searches and smells about, it is not quiet for a moment, it trusts nothing until it has examined and made acquaintance with everything.*

*Free people, remember this maxim: We may acquire liberty, but it is never recovered if it is once lost.*

CHAPTER SIXTEEN

# Arthur Schopenhauer

**(1788–1860)**

- Asserted "will" as principle of all life
- Viewed life in pessimistic fashion
- Tried to bridge world of experience and world of nature

Arthur Schopenhauer was as brilliant as he was pessimistic. His views may not make you proud to be a human being, but they are fascinating and inspired many generations of thinkers to come, especially Nietzsche.

Schopenhauer's father was a wealthy merchant in Danzig. His mother was a popular novelist. Schopenhauer disliked commercial pursuits and turned to the study of philosophy. An avid traveler, Schopenhauer visited most of the countries of Western Europe. He studied philosophy, natural science, and Sanskrit literature at the University of Berlin, where he eventually lectured. He disliked the popular Hegelianism of the day, and found his inspiration in Plato and Kant. His fame was a long time coming, and he spent his last years thinking and writing in Frankfort-on-the-Main. He died in 1860.

## Schopenhauer's Big Idea #1: Assert Your Will

For Schopenhauer, Kant had it right when he said that the world of experience is conditioned by the forms of the mind (space and time). Kant maintained we cannot have certain knowledge of "things in themselves" outside of our experience of them. Schopenhauer sought to bridge the gap left by Kant's distinction between phenomenon (the stuff of experience) and *noumenon* (things in themselves).

The absolute principle of the world for Schopenhauer is Will. This Will is spaceless, timeless, and completely without cause. In lower life forms, it is simply the blind will of self-preservation. But for humans, the Will seeks to attain consciousness. Once the Will has attained consciousness in the human brain, the world becomes an Idea or representation. This representation is our experience of that world, in which everything is recognized as being Will. The Will is the "thing in itself"—both the representation of the world and how the world actually is.

The Will is the fundamental principle of the external world, and we, as a body, are part of that will. Our essential nature is that of Will and our bodies, like the entire external world, are just expressions of that universal principle of life. Will is everywhere and everything is guided by it. It expresses itself as yearning and craving in humankind, and even is the principle of our perception; we perceive what we Will to perceive. In other words, the essential principle of the world is not a thing such as water (Thales' idea). Rather, the principle of the world "will," which moves nature through purely physical operations, becomes, in man, a consciousness that exhibits itself as "striving" or "craving" and an instinct for self-preservation.

**Bessie is me. I am Bessie.**

Bessie the Cow is Will just as I am Will. But this principle is only a blind drive for self-preservation in her, where it has become consciousness in me. But essentially, my nature is the same as hers; we are both part of the universal principle of life. We are both part of Will.

## Schopenhauer's Big Idea #2: The Schopenhauer Ethic

Will is the will to live, the will to be, and thus the cause of all suffering in the world. For Schopenhauer, the Will in man makes him intriguing, selfish, and grasping. He believes that life is essentially evil. The paradox of existence is that the essential principle is the will to live, which is absolutely defeated in death. Schopenhauer (a cheerful guy, as you can already tell) is big on death. Death will conquer all. This world is the worst of all possible worlds, for the very principle of existence (Will) is inevitably defeated in the individual by death.

If life is essentially base and selfish, a moral act will be one that is based not on some strange principle or some abstract idea of justice—it will be committed out of sympathy. A moral act is always unselfish.

### Bessie Meets Schopenhauer II

To kill Bessie for sport is wrong because it is just a selfish act that only satisfies my desire for fun. This kind of moral reasoning is very similar to the Eastern religious teachings of Buddhism and Taoism. After all, Schopenhauer studied Sanskrit literature and Eastern religion, and this kind of moral view is similar to those traditions.

While his views may be seen as depressing to you and me, Schopenhauer's effect on future thinkers, especially Nietzsche, was simply huge. He asserted the universal principle of Will to discover the "things in themselves" outside our experience, and inspired future generations of philosophers.

*To overcome difficulties is to experience the full delight of existence.*

*To marry is to halve your rights and double your duties.*

*The greatest of follies is to sacrifice health for any other kind of happiness.*

*All truth passes through three stages. First, it is ridiculed. Second, it is violently opposed. Third, it is accepted as being self-evident.*

*Fame is something that must be won. Honor is something that must not be lost.*

*It is with trifles and when he is off guard that a man best reveals his character.*

*Buying books would be a good thing if one could also buy the time to read them in: But as a rule the purchase of books is mistaken for the appropriation of their contents.*

*Religion is the masterpiece of the art of animal training, for it trains people as to how they shall think.*

*Everyone takes the limits of his own vision for the limits of the world.*

*Compassion is the basis of all morality.*

*Noise is the most impertinent of all forms of interruption. It is not only an interruption, but is also a disruption of thought.*

*The memory should be specially taxed in youth, since it is then that it is strongest and most tenacious. But in choosing the things that should be committed to memory the utmost care and forethought must be exercised; as lessons well learnt in youth are never forgotten.*

*We forfeit three-fourths of ourselves to be like other people.*

*Every nation ridicules other nations—and all are right.*

*If we weren't all so interested in ourselves, life would be so uninteresting we couldn't endure it.*

*The closing years of life are like the end of a masquerade party when the masks are dropped.*

*A man can do what he wants, but not want what he wants.*

*If you want to know your true opinion of someone, watch the effect produced in you by the first sight of a letter from him.*

*Talent hits a target no one else can hit; Genius hits a target no one else can see.*
*With people with only modest ability, modesty is mere honesty; but with those who possess great talent it is hypocrisy.*

CHAPTER SEVENTEEN

# John Stuart Mill

**(1806-1873)**

- Most famous and influential "utilitarian"
- Great advocate of social change and women's rights
- Asserted importance of individual liberty and free speech

The nineteenth century gave rise to many important political thinkers, as well as much-needed political reform. It was much like the 1960s in this way, except that the popular clothes of the day were infinitely more pleasing to the eye. John Stuart Mill was a product of this century, and following in the footsteps of other English thinkers, such as John Locke,

Mill's influence on our modern conceptions of "individualism" and "liberty" are nothing short of profound.

John Stuart Mill was born the son of James and Harriet Mill in London. Mill's father was a tough-minded man who subjected his son to a relentless philosophical curriculum. By the age of ten, Mill had learned Latin and Greek, and had written summaries of Plato's theories. While this rigorous education certainly benefited his intellectual development, it just may not have been the best way to grow up. Between this intense education and his unfeeling father, Mill concluded later in his life that, "I was never a boy."

By the time Mill was seventeen he earned a reputation as an active political thinker, publishing articles and the like. He advocated for social reform based on the "Utilitarian" perspective his father had introduced to him. But at twenty Mill suffered a breakdown and went through a major depression. He said he had "never learned to feel." Mill turned to reading poetry to stir his soul. Eventually, he met Harriet Taylor in 1831 and fell in love. She would prove a great influence on Mill's philosophy, especially contributing to his liberal feminism. They lived happily ever after in France, where he died in 1873.

Although Mill is not the "father" of Utilitarianism, he is certainly the most famous of its advocates. Mill accepted Utilitarianism but argued for a more qualitative understanding, and not just quantitative. So, then, what the heck is Utilitarianism?

## Mill's Big Idea: Utilitarianism

Following in the tradition of Hume and Locke, Mill accepted their empiricist conception of knowledge. Thus it follows that moral theory cannot be based on abstract notions such as "duty" or "conscience" like Kant asserted—instead it must be based on the maximization of pleasure and the minimization of pain—that is, the promotion of happiness. Since happiness is the goal of human behavior, Utilitarianism suggests that laws and actions are "good" if they provide "the greatest happiness for the greatest number." Actions are "good" or "bad" depending upon how "useful" they are in the pursuit of happiness. "Useful" equals "utility" equals "Utilitarianism."

More than advocating and modifying the utilitarian moral view, Mill strongly asserts the importance of absolute individual rights that must be protected by the State. The individual's right to free speech, for example, should never be silenced. *No matter how happy or pleasurable a million people find it.* Mill protects the rights of the individual more than any philosopher before him.

## Bessie Gets Utilitarian

Bessie and her cow friends decide to pass a law not to step on each other's hooves. While there is nothing "intrinsically good" about this law, it provides the utility of maximizing all the cows' ability to graze safely without interruption and usurpation of their private space.

While Mill agrees with this basic method of determining "good" actions, he focuses more on the concepts of individual rights and liberties than his utilitarian predecessors. He also stresses the quality of the pleasure and pain as a standard of determination.

For example, while Bessie might find a great quantity of happiness or pleasure by eating grass all day, the quality of this pleasure and experience are questionable. "Better to be a dissatisfied human being than a satisfied pig," Mill famously remarks. It is not only the quantity of pleasure but the quality that are both taken into account in Mill's view.

*One person with a belief is equal to a force of ninety-nine who have only interests.*

*Though the practice of chivalry fell even more sadly short of its theoretic standard than practice generally falls below theory, it remains one of the most precious monuments of the moral history of our race, as a remarkable instance of a concerted and organized attempt by a most disorganized and distracted society, to raise up and carry into practice a moral ideal greatly in advance of its social condition and institutions; so much so as to have been completely frustrated in the main object, yet never entirely inefficacious, and which has left a most sensible, and for the most part a highly valuable impress on the ideas and feelings of all subsequent times.*

*They who know how to employ opportunities will often find that they can create them; and what we can achieve depends less on the amount of time we possess than on the use we make of our time.*

*The peculiar evil of silencing the expression of an opinion is that it is robbing the human race; posterity as well as the existing generation; those who dissent from the opinion, still more than those who hold it. If the opinion is right, they are deprived of the opportunity of exchanging error for truth: if wrong, they lose, what is almost as great a benefit, the clearer perception and livelier impression of truth, produced by its collision with error.*

*No stronger case can be shown for prohibiting anything which is regarded as a personal immorality, than is made out for suppressing these practices in the eyes of those who regard them as impieties; and unless we are willing to adopt the logic of persecutors, and to say that we may persecute others because we are right, and that they must not persecute us because they are wrong, we must be aware of admitting a principle of which we should resent as a gross injustice the application to ourselves.*

*A man who has nothing which he cares about more than he does about his personal safety is a miserable creature who has no chance of being free, unless made and kept so by the existing of better men than himself.*

*Truth gains more even by the errors of one who, with due study, and preparation, thinks for himself, than by the true opinions of those who only hold them because they do not suffer themselves to think.*

*No one can be a great thinker who does not recognize that as a thinker it is his first duty to follow his intellect to whatever conclusions it may lead.*

*Truth gains more even by the errors of one who, with due study, and preparation, thinks for himself, than by the true opinions of those who only hold them because they do not suffer themselves to think.*

*Ask yourself whether you are happy and you cease to be so.*

*He who lets the world, or his own portion of it, choose his plan of life for him, has no need of any other faculty than the ape-like one of imitation. He who chooses his plan for himself, employs all his faculties. He must use observation to see, reasoning and judgment to foresee, activity to gather materials for decision, discrimination to decide, and when he has decided, firmness and self-control to hold to his deliberate decision.*

*The only freedom which deserves the name is that of pursuing our own good in our own way, so long as we do not attempt to deprive others of theirs, or impede their efforts to obtain it. Each is the proper guardian of his own health, whether bodily, or mental or spiritual. Mankind are greater gainers by suffering each other to live as seems good to themselves, than by compelling each to live as seems good to the rest.*

*The general tendency of things throughout the world is to render mediocrity the ascendant power among mankind.*

*A party of order or stability, and a party of progress or reform, are both necessary elements of a healthy state of political life.*
*That so few now dare to be eccentric, marks the chief danger of the time.*

*He who knows only his own side of the case knows little of that.*

*The pupil who is never required to do what he cannot do, never does what he can do.*

*There are many truths of which the full meaning cannot be realized until personal experience has brought it home.*

*Indeed the dictum that truth always triumphs over persecution, is one of those pleasant falsehoods which men repeat after one another til they pass into common places, but which all experience refutes.*

*If mankind minus one were of one opinion, then mankind is no more justified in silencing the one than the one—if he had the power—would be justified in silencing mankind.*

*War is an ugly thing, but not the ugliest of things. The decayed and degraded state of moral and patriotic feeling which thinks that nothing is worth war is much worse. The person who has nothing for which he is willing to fight, nothing which is more important than his own personal safety, is a miserable creature and has no chance of being free unless made and kept so by the exertions of better men than himself.*

*A person may cause evil to others not only by his actions but by his inaction, and in either case he is justly accountable to them for the injury.*

*The only purpose for which power can be rightfully exercised over any member of a civilized community, against his will, is to prevent harm to others. His own good, either physical or moral, is not a sufficient warrant.*

*As long as justice and injustice have not terminated their ever renewing fight for ascendancy in the affairs of mankind, human beings must be willing, when need is, to do battle for the one against the other.*

*No slave is a slave to the same lengths, and in so full a sense of the word, as a wife is.*

*Marriage is the only actual bondage known to our law. There remain no legal slaves, except the mistress of every house.*

*Conservatives are not necessarily stupid, but most stupid people are conservatives.*

CHAPTER EIGHTEEN

# Søren Kierkegaard

**(1813–1855)**

- Father of "Existentialism"
- Focused on the aspects of the individual life
- Advocated a "leap of faith" to release the anxiety of human freedom

Søren Kierkegaard's work expresses the modern anxiety of the individual trying to find and discover meaning in life. He is to philosophy what Woody Allen is to film. But basically, he's not quite as funny.

Kierkegaard was born in Copenhagen, Denmark. Like Mill, Kierkegaard received a rigorous homeschooling in philosophy. But unlike Mill's father, Kierkegaard's father was deeply religious, emotional, and possibly disturbed. A successful merchant, he nonetheless believed that God had cursed him and his family and condemned them to suffering.

While studying theology at the University of Copenhagen, Kierkegaard strongly opposed the popular Hegelian philosophy of his day. He believed that its lack of individualism and its systematic nature should not tell an individual how to live or what to do.

Not that Kierkegaard knew how to live or what to do with himself. He was well-liked by others for his wit, charm, and affable nature—but when this social butterfly was alone, he was often seriously depressed. Seeking meaning in his life, Kierkegaard became a Lutheran pastor and got married. But this did not satisfy him, and he lost interest both in marriage and in organized religion. He got a divorce and spent the rest of his short life publishing works under various pseudonyms. Remaining unknown, Kierkegaard collapsed on the street and died in 1855. His works would not be read and appreciated for decades to come—when Kierkegaard would be regarded as the "father" of Existentialism.

## Kierkegaard's Big Idea #1: Existentialism

Kierkegaard asserted that there is no inherent purpose in the world that can be understood or proved by rational exposition. Unlike what Hegel or Aristotle believed, the world and the life in it have no purpose, Kierkegaard said. In addition, God cannot be proved by rational expression. None of these things can be proved. The universe is unexplainable. More than that, a philosophy like Hegel's, which deals with these metaphysical issues, doesn't serve as a guide to life for an individual. One thing philosophy can explain, according to Kierkegaard, is that we are isolated individuals, and that we have the ability to *choose* one thing over another. The uniqueness of human experience is that we are each an isolated creature with the capacity to make choices because of our free will.

This freedom to choose creates anxiety within us, leading to feelings of isolation. Thus Kierkegaard advises that we each take a "leap of faith." Literally, to choose that life must matter even though we can't prove it. Kierkegaard says this even though he acknowledges that "rational proof" of God is impossible.

Kierkegaard's existentialism focuses on what it means to be an individual and how to lead a fulfilling life. He disparages "objective truth," claiming that the "subjective truth" is the one that counts. His main point: **What we believe does not matter as much as how we believe it.** This is the heart of existentialism.

## Kierkegaard's Big Idea #2: The Three Stages of Living

Kierkegaard's philosophy is grounded in individual actualization and self-fulfillment. There are three different stages of self-actualization.

1) The aesthetic: This stage of life is centered around the hedonist's drive for pleasure and instant gratification. In this stage, you live only for the present and thus limit the scope and meaning of your existence. The result: A life of boredom and an avoidance of real decisions. But, as Woody Allen says, while "sex without love is an empty experience, as empty experiences go, it's one of the best."
2) The ethical: This stage is characterized as the stage in which you commit to universal principles and moral standards to guide your behavior—and bingo!—your life has more scope and meaning. Still, this is not sufficient to achieve self-actualization.
3) The religious: This is the final stage of self-actualization. You give up "ethical principles" for a passionate and complete devotion to God. Only in this stage of passionate reverie are you relatively free from the anxiety of human existence.

Kierkegaard, while not recognized in his own time, had a tremendous impact on philosophy, fueling a whole genre of philosophical thought called "Existentialism." If it doesn't matter *what* we believe, just as long as we believe in *something* to make life meaningful, maybe I'll stop telling my senile grandfather that he's wrong to believe that the highest good man can attain is the breeding of excellent homing pigeons.

### Bessie Gets Ethical

Johnny the Farmer loves Bessie the Cow. Not in an illegal way, but she is his favorite cow on the farm. God speaks to Johnny and tells him to cut her throat. Although God is all-knowing and all-powerful, Johnny hesitates, because he has an inclination to be ethical. However, he doesn't do the ethical thing; his faith in God and His moral insight compels him to prepare for Bessie's death. As in the biblical story of Abraham and Isaac, Johnny's faith has been proven and God then allows Bessie to live. What is the point? The passionate reverie, trust, and faith in God that Johnny exhibits causes him to "suspend the ethical." This suspension is the height of self-actualization and the highest level of meaning that humans can achieve.

*People demand freedom of speech to make up for the freedom of thought which they avoid.*

*Far from idleness being the root of all evil, it is rather the only true good.*

*Most people are subjective towards themselves and objective towards all others, frightfully objective sometimes—but the task is precisely to be objective towards oneself and subjective towards all others.*

*Life can only be understood backwards; but it must be lived forwards.*

*Most men pursue pleasure with such breathless haste that they hurry past it.*

*The paradox of Christian truth is invariable, due to the fact that it is the truth that exists for God. The standard of measure and the end is super-human; and there is only one relationship possible: faith.*

*There are men who are wanting in the comparative, they as a rule are the most interesting.*

*It takes moral courage to grieve, it takes religious courage to rejoice.*

*This is all that I have known for certain, that God is love. Even if I have mistaken this or that point: God is nevertheless love.*

*Genius, like that of a thunderstorm, comes up against the wind.*

*What is a poet, an unhappy person who conceals profound anguish in his heart but whose lips are so formed that as sighs and cries pass over them they sound like beautiful music.*

*If a man cannot forget, he will never amount to much.*

*Life is not a problem to be solved, but a reality to be experienced.*

*I am so stupid that I cannot understand philosophy, the antithesis of this is that philosophy is so clever that it cannot comprehend my stupidity. These antitheses are mediated in a higher unity; in our common stupidity.*

*In addition to my other numerous acquaintances, I have one more intimate confidant. My depression is the most faithful mistress I have known—no wonder, then, that I return the love.*

*Prayer does not change God, but changes him who prays.*

*Life has its own hidden forces which you can only discover by living.*

CHAPTER NINETEEN

# Friedrich Nietzsche

**(1844-1900)**

- Declared the "death of God"
- Sought to transform human values
- Asserted idea of "Will to power"

Frederick Nietzsche is one of the most widely read and beloved philosophers. His poetic style captivates as much as it educates its readers.

Nietzsche was born in Rocken, Prussia. His father, a Lutheran minister, died when he was only five. From then on, Nietzsche was raised by a household of women. Nietzsche eventually went on to the famous boarding school at Pforta, where he did excellent work despite the horrible migraines and nausea that plagued him then and throughout his life. At the University of Bonn, Nietzsche studied classical philology (linguistics) and theology. During the first year, Nietzsche lost his religious faith as well as his interest in theology. He subsequently transferred to the University of Leipzig to continue his studies in philology. Just based on his papers at that school, Nietzsche was recommended for a professorship at the University of Basel at the remarkably young age of 29.

Nietzsche wrote his philosophy while teaching at the university, until his deteriorating health forced him to quit in 1879. He spent the next decade traveling to different places in search of a desirable climate. These years of travel and sickness, however, were some of his most productive years as a philosopher. In 1888, Nietzsche began to show signs of madness, and in 1889 he collapsed in Turin, Italy.

Due to the aphoristic nature of his philosophical writing, Nietzsche has been widely interpreted and misunderstood. Part of this misunderstanding comes from his sister, a rabid anti-Semite and Nazi enthusiast who published her subjectively-edited version of his last works after his death. Nietzsche himself had broken off relations with people over their anti-Semitic views, most notably his friend, composer Richard Wagner.

## Nietzsche's Big Idea #1: Slave vs. Noble Morality

One of Nietzsche's goals was to trace the historical development of what he called "slave morality." In early times, the ancient Greeks considered an action "good" if it was noble, powerful, beautiful, or of an excellent standard. "Bad" was the contrary of "good." A bad action was lowly, without greatness. These values were life-affirming and a worthwhile standard, according to Nietzsche.

But this changed with the Jews and then with the Christians. By looking for values that could not be denied on their own terms, that is, by attributing them to a God outside of themselves, the "good" became identified with ideas such as pity and humility. These values were born out of resentment for the powerful and the noble. This resentment was essentially a resentment of humanity and all of its capabilities. They were essentially negative, and it is with these moral notions that "bad" became not the opposite of an Ideal, but a transformation into an idea of the sinful, evil, and ungodly. Nietzsche's story of moral development was one of bewitchment and castigation, where "slave morality" was used as a kind of spiritual revenge.

Yep, you guessed it. Nietzsche called for a "transformation of values." These values were to be based on the concepts of "noble morality." The first step in this process was to proclaim the "death of God," for with his death, we will free ourselves from the "slave morality" that is dependent upon Him. If you're the genius who can complete this "transformation of values," you become the "Overman" (Übermensch). You will lead human beings to a life without resentment. You'll be the antithesis of

God, transcending your human form and bringing human beings beyond good and evil by exercising your "will to power."

## Nietzsche's Big Idea #2: The Will to Power

According to Nietzsche, every human relationship is a power struggle. Both moral codes (slave and noble), for example, were created to exercise power over others. Therefore, all human behavior is a result of the "will to power." But, while the hero in ancient myth asserts his "master morality" by taking direct action over the weaker opponent, the Judeo-Christian "slave morality" asserts itself with deep conceptions of revenge, pity, and eternal suffering.

But Nietzsche suggested we focus less on the desire to overcome others, and more on our individual need to overcome our animal instincts and re-invent ourselves. This is a process of self-actualization, to gain self-power and shape our passions, impulses, and character.

Due to this strange talk about "will to power" and his sister's anti-Semitic editing, Nietzsche was championed by the Nazis. But Nietzsche championed the individual above all else, and his concern is really about the fulfillment of individual existence. In this, he became a great inspiration to many existentialist writers in the twentieth century. Damn Nazis, gotta try and ruin everything.

**Bessie's Will to Power**

For example, Nietzsche talks a lot about the "herd mentality." If Bessie is going to reach any kind of self-actualization, she must break away from the herd of her fellow cows and ignore the moral teachings they have

been poisoned with. Break way Bess, and create your identity. It's up to you girl, whether you will be a weak or a strong cow. Exercise the *will to power* within.

*We love life, not because we are used to living but because we are used to loving.*

*People who have given us their complete confidence believe that they have a right to ours. The inference is false, a gift confers no rights.*

*Does wisdom perhaps appear on the earth as a raven which is inspired by the smell of carrion?*

*At times one remains faithful to a cause only because its opponents do not cease to be insipid.*

*A woman may very well form a friendship with a man, but for this to endure, it must be assisted by a little physical antipathy.*

*Whoever fights monsters should see to it that in the process he does not become a monster. And if you gaze long enough into an abyss, the abyss will gaze back into you.*

*Talking much about oneself can also be a means to conceal oneself.*

*There are no facts, only interpretations.*

*One often contradicts an opinion when what is uncongenial is really the tone in which it was conveyed.*

*Family love is messy, clinging, and of an annoying and repetitive pattern, like bad wallpaper.*

*Without music, life would be a mistake.*

*The Christian resolution to find the world ugly and bad has made the world ugly and bad.*

*It is hard enough to remember my opinions, without also remembering my reasons for them!*

*On the mountains of truth you can never climb in vain: Either you will reach a point higher up today, or you will be training your powers so that you will be able to climb higher tomorrow.*

*Every extension of knowledge arises from making the conscious the unconscious.*

*In individuals, insanity is rare; but in groups, parties, nations, and epochs it is the rule.*

*Wisdom sets bounds even to knowledge.*

*What does not destroy me, makes me stronger.*

*Man is the cruelest animal.*

*What someone is, begins to be revealed when his talent abates, when he stops showing us what he can do.*

*Under peaceful conditions, the militant man attacks himself.*

*To forget one's purpose is the commonest form of stupidity.*

*The miserable have no other medicine but hope.*

*The doer alone learneth.*

*Faith is not wanting to know what is true.*

*The best friend is likely to acquire the best wife, because a good marriage is based on the talent for friendship.*

*Success has always been a great liar.*

*One should die proudly when it is no longer possible to live proudly.*

*Not by wrath does one kill, but by laughter.*

CHAPTER TWENTY

# John Dewey

**(1859–1953)**

- Considered to be the most distinguished advocate of Pragmatism
- Asserted the philosophy of Instrumentalism
- His "democratic" conception of education revolutionized the public school system

In the nineteenth century, there was a very influential and important philosophical tradition called Pragmatism developing in the United States. Although not invented by Dewey, he is to Pragmatism what John Stuart Mill is to Utilitarianism, that is, its most influential and distinguished advocate.

John Dewey was born in Burlington, Vermont. He was descended from a long line of Vermont farmers, and no Dewey had ever been to college. His father was content with a simple life, but Dewey's mother tried to encourage intellectual curiosity and religious sentiment in her young son. He entered the University of Vermont in 1875, studying mostly natural science and philosophy. After college, Dewey taught in high schools while writing several important philosophical articles. He then went back to school, eventually getting a doctorate from Johns Hopkins University.

As a well-known philosopher, he wrote about more things than you can count, most notably democracy, education, and culture. His popularity accounts for the number of John Dewey high schools across America.

John Dewey continued to write and to influence the social institutions of his time, while teaching at Columbia University from 1904 to 1930. Although famous and widely respected, Dewey upheld his father's tradition of valuing the simple life. He retired on Long Island, managed a small egg farm, and eventually died in 1952.

## Dewey's Big Idea: Instrumentalism

Dewey's philosophy of Instrumentalism comes out of the tradition of Pragmatism. The basic principle of Pragmatism: You find truth when you consider the practical consequence of a given idea. Thus truth changes depending on the situation; there is no abstract metaphysical eternal *truth*. Dewey believes philosophy is a practical tool for solving social problems.

Dewey's Instrumentalism contends that ideas are instruments of the mind used to realize purposes, purposes we can use to cope with a given situation. We should rid ourselves of the metaphysical; philosophy should not concern itself with the metaphysical (God, universal principles, atoms, etc.) for these only have *reality* and importance in the struggles of human beings and the problems of social life. The truth of something should be considered as a hypothesis, and tested in a given situation to determine the utility and merit of the thesis. In this view, the only kind of knowledge that is reasonably attainable is a kind of problem-solving knowledge.

For example, *we* cannot know whether Bessie and her cow friends have immortal souls, so we should concern ourselves with the problems of cow life and whether Bessie eats too much grass.

Since reality is always changing, philosophy should explore and adapt to specific economic and social issues. Just as human cognition itself is an instrument used to cope with a given situation or problem, so should philosophy be used as an instrument for social and political change.

Dewey says that we should test our moral notions and, based on the consequences, either use them or dismiss them. Weary of notions that are considered to be fixed or eternal by nature, Dewey advises an experimental approach to morality. Just like truth, moral precepts are fallible and need to be tested in different situations.

Dewey applied his philosophy to almost every discipline imaginable. His influence on education was especially profound, and his ideas that learning and the discovery of truth should be based on testing and experience, rather than on abstract and inapplicable notions, has had a lasting impact on education. Dewey called for an end to the idea that education should simply prepare students for civil life through a dogmatic program of crude memorization. Instead, he believed that education should fully integrate and encourage student participation based on the notion that students were already an extension of civil life. He called for an emphasis on the creation and cultivation of "democratic habits" such as cooperation and community participation from students of the earliest ages.

As social problems constantly change, Dewey held that, due to the flexibility and adaptability of democracy, it was of primary ethical value. So democracy is the best form of government there is. Well, now that's what I call pragmatic thinking.

*Every serious-minded person knows that a large part of the effort required in moral discipline consists in the courage needed to acknowledge the unpleasant consequences of one's past and present acts.*

*Education is a social process; education is growth; education is not a preparation for life but is life itself.*

*There is more than a verbal tie between the words common, community, and communication. Try the experiment of communicating, with fullness and accuracy, some experience to another, especially if it be somewhat complicated, and you will find your own attitude toward your experience changing.*

*Intellectually, religious emotions are not creative but conservative. They attach themselves readily to the current view of the world and consecrate it.*

*Luck, bad if not good, will always be with us. But it has a way of favoring the intelligent and showing its back to the stupid.*

*It is our American habit if we find the foundations of our educational structure unsatisfactory to add another story or wing. We find it easier to add a new study or course or kind of school than to recognize existing conditions so as to meet the need.*

*We cannot seek or attain health, wealth, learning, justice or kindness in general. Action is always specific, concrete, individualized, unique.*

*Education is life itself.*

*Confidence is directness and courage in meeting the facts of life.*

*Anyone who has begun to think, places some portion of the world in jeopardy.*

*Arriving at one goal is the starting point to another.*

*Conflict is the gadfly of thought. It stirs us to observation and memory. It instigates to invention. It shocks us out of sheeplike passivity, and sets us at noting and contriving.*

*By reading the characteristic features of any man's castles in the air you can make a shrewd guess as to his underlying desires which are frustrated.*

*Every great advance in science has issued from a new audacity of imagination.*

*Failure is instructive. The person who really thinks learns quite as much from his failures as from his successes. Genuine ignorance is profitable because it is likely to be accompanied by humility, curiosity, and open-mindedness; whereas ability to repeat catch-phrases, cant terms, familiar propositions, gives the conceit of learning and coats the mind with varnish waterproof to new ideas.*

*Just as a flower which seems beautiful and has color but no perfume, so are the fruitless words of the man who speaks them but does them not.*

*No man's credit is as good as his money.*

*One lives with so many bad deeds on one's conscience and some good intentions in one's heart.*

*The self is not something ready-made, but something in continuous formation through choice of action.*

*Time and memory are true artists; they remould reality nearer to the heart's desire.*

*To find out what one is fitted to do, and to secure an opportunity to do it, is the key to happiness.*

*To me faith means not worrying.*

*A democracy is more than a form of government; it is primarily a mode of associated living, of conjoint communicated experience.*

*The method of democracy is to bring conflicts out into the open where their special claims can be seen and appraised, where they can be discussed and judged.*

CHAPTER TWENTY-ONE

# Ludwig Wittgenstein

**(1889–1951)**

- **Influential analytic philosopher**
- **Saw language as a game**
- **Believed philosophical problems result from misuse of language**

Ludwig Wittgenstein revolutionized the philosophical world in the twentieth century.

Born in Vienna, Wittgenstein was one of eight children in a very wealthy and prominent family. Though his ancestry was Jewish, his family had converted to Roman Catholicism.

Before becoming interested in philosophy, Wittgenstein studied mathematics with the intention of becoming an aeronautical engineer. His studies led him from the University of Berlin to the University of Manchester in England. In Manchester, he became very interested in the foundation of mathematics rather than engineering. This interest led him to the University of Cambridge where he met and studied with one of the pioneers of analytic philosophy, Bertrand Russell.

At the outbreak of World War I, Wittgenstein moved back to Austria and joined the war effort. As he fought on the relatively quiet Italian Front, he began his doctoral dissertation, a paper that would become one of the most influential philosophical works of the last century.

But his success and fame did not make him the happiest of men. Throughout his life he would be very conflicted by his homosexuality, and often repressed it. This conflict contributed to his serious depression. He came close to committing suicide on several occasions.

After the war, Wittgenstein decided to become a schoolteacher. He gave away all the fortune his family bestowed upon him. In 1925, Wittgenstein quit teaching schoolchildren, and worked at odd jobs. In 1929, he returned to Cambridge to lecture, where his deeply charismatic and idiosyncratic teaching style drew many fascinated disciples. He spent the rest of his life teaching and writing philosophy, until his death in 1951.

Wittgenstein's first contribution to philosophy was influenced by his mentor Bertrand Russell, and shared his basic principles. The task of the analytic philosopher was to create a kind of "Ideal" logical language, which, once completed, would serve to mirror the *reality* of the world. Since analytical philosophers believed the world could be understood mathematically, Russell tried to represent the laws of arithmetic in logical language. Basically, analytic philosophers believed there is a "reality" of the world, and that philosophy should create a new science of logic that corresponds directly to it.

## Wittgenstein's Big Idea #1: Reality As a Picture

Wittgenstein focused on the relationship between our minds, the language we use, and reality. According to Wittgenstein's first philosophical view, there is a direct, logical correspondence between objects in reality, thoughts in the human mind, and language.

For instance, if I say that Bessie the Cow is an idiot, the insult must have direct reference to an external object or it would have no meaning whatsoever. That is to say, to know and speak about a cow is to be able to picture a cow. A statement or preposition derives its meaning from its necessary logical relation to *reality*. Furthermore, every proposition, like the example I gave, forms a picture in the mind. Language and the mind form a kind of picture of the reality they correspond to in the world. All the facts of the world are facts because we can speak and picture them. In other words, facts correspond to a word in language that, in turn, corresponds to some kind of mental representation.

Language and thought only have meaning insofar as they correspond directly and logically to reality. This means that metaphysical entities cannot be discussed or philosophically investigated because the only tool we can use for the discussion is the language we use. Then, because a language derives its meaning from the reality it corresponds to, it is forced to correspond directly to the facts of the world. If it doesn't correspond to the *actual facts of the world*, then it is not a logical language, and therefore has no meaning.

Without this perfect representational language, metaphysics and the philosophical investigation of justice or morality is impossible. These are concepts that cannot be **pictured** and therefore do not correspond to **real facts**. So, while the concepts of justice and morality exist, it would be impossible to discover their actual nature.

## Wittgenstein's Big Idea #2: Language As a Game

Interestingly, Wittgenstein's final philosophical enquiries led him to reject his former views. Instead, his next big claim was that words in ordinary language sometimes only bear a "family resemblance" to one another and that meaning of words is due to the interrelated nature of language. Just as a move on the chessboard only has meaning insofar as it relates to all the moves before (it has no meaning in and of itself), some words derive their stable meaning from the "language game."

Take a joke, for example. A joke's meaning is dependent upon all the "moves" that could have been made or have been made. We need to know what could have been said, or what is usually said, or a variety of other language associations in order for the joke to have meaning. This necessary knowledge of what cannot and can be said often gives statements and words their meaning.

Basically, Wittgenstein began to see language not as corresponding to anything "real," but as a set of rules that humans adopt, much like that of a game. Even something like arithmetic, according to Wittgenstein's later position, does not have a direct correspondence to reality. It is just a way that society communicates.

For example, the equation 2+2=4 is nothing more than a kind of language game we have decided to share for the purposes of human life; it represents nothing in **reality** whatsoever. With this point of view, his former attempt to understand the world through a new science of logic is completely impossible.

In the end, it was Wittgenstein's view that the truth of a statement cannot be understood in its relation to an external or "language-independent" reality, because that reality presents itself only in the linguistic forms that we have constructed.

Wittgenstein's influence is extraordinary because he left this science with only one legitimate task: To pay attention to the use of language so that the philosophical problems caused by the misuse of words can be avoided. So I guess we are back to square one in terms of many philosophical problems. *But it doesn't even make sense to talk about them!*

*Whereof one cannot speak, thereof one must be silent.*

*I don't know why we are here, but I'm pretty sure that it is not in order to enjoy ourselves.*

*Philosophy is a battle against the bewitchment of our intelligence by means of language.*

*The world of the happy is quite different from that of the unhappy.*

*There is no religious denomination in which the misuse of metaphysical expressions has been responsible for so much sin as it has in mathematics.*

*Genius is what makes us forget the master's talent.*

*We could present spatially an atomic fact which contradicted the laws of physics, but not one which contradicted the laws of geometry.*

*There can never be surprises in logic.*

*The riddle does not exist. If a question can be put at all, then it can also be answered.*

*Everything that can be said, can be said clearly.*

*All mathematics is tautology.*

*The process of calculating brings about just this intuition. Calculation is not an experiment.*

*A mathematical proof must be perspicuous.*

*The limits of my language mean the limits of my world.*

*With my full philosophical rucksack I can only climb slowly up the mountain of mathematics.*

*No one can think a thought for me in the way that no one can don my hat for me.*

*Telling someone something he does not understand is pointless, even if you add that he will not be able to understand it.*

*What Copernicus really achieved was not the discovery of a true theory but of a fertile new point of view.*

*If it is true that words have meanings, why don't we throw away words and keep just the meanings?*

*The popular scientific books by our scientists aren't the outcome of hard work, but are written when they are resting on their laurels.*

*It's a question of envy of course. And anyone who experiences it ought to keep on telling himself: "It's a mistake! It's a mistake!"*

*Death is not an event in life; we do not experience death.*

*Even when all the possible scientific questions have been answered, the problems of life remain completely untouched.*

CHAPTER TWENTY-TWO

# Jean-Paul Sartre

**(1905–1980)**

- **Humans are free and responsible**
- **There is no abstract human nature**
- **Self-deception leads to acting in "bad faith"**

When we think of existentialism in the twentieth century, we no doubt think of Sartre. After two World Wars, Western civilization had proven itself morally bankrupt; in this context, Sartre stressed the importance of human freedom and moral responsibility. His philosophy expressed itself in award-winning novels and plays, as well as philosophical texts.

Jean-Paul Sartre was born in Paris, France. His father was a naval officer. Sartre was a curious young lad, always poking his nose into any book he could find. Eventually, he would interest himself in philosophy. Sartre traveled and continued his philosophy studies all over Europe and Egypt. At the outbreak of World War II in 1939, Sartre served in the French army. A year later, he was captured by the Germans, spending over nine months in a German POW camp. In 1941, he escaped and joined the French Resistance. From 1941 to 1944, Sartre would earn a reputation as a prominent figure in this movement, writing for its underground newspapers on a regular basis.

After the war, Sartre taught at universities and wrote famous and influential philosophy and literature. He continued to be a vocal supporter of freedom around the world, condemning acts of aggression wherever he saw them. When he died in 1980, he was one of the most respected leaders of post-war France.

## Sartre's Big Idea: Existentialism

Like Kierkegaard, Sartre believes that the starting point of philosophy is the subjective, and there is no "objective truth" attainable by humankind. However, Sartre differs from Kierkegaard in that he is an atheist, claiming that there is no reason to take Kierkegaard's "leap of faith." Meaning must be found solely through the essence of what it is to be an individual free-will. That is to say, the meaning of life starts and ends with the meaning of the individual, whose essential nature is defined completely by the choices he freely chooses to make. In the Sartrian brand of existentialism, morality and the very meaning of what it is to be a person are the products ( not the productive force) of the individual human ability to "choose freely."

This idea is opposite to the claim of an objective and absolute "human nature". As Hobbes thought, human nature was characterized by a constant striving for power (as did Nietzsche), and Hegel thought that an objective spirit of freedom becomes historically embodied in subjective consciousness, Sartre and the existentialists claim that "what it is to be human" is completely determined by our ability as free-willed agents to choose freely. Most importantly for Sartre, our moral values are brought into the world through our actions and our choices. The universe itself is wholly without value and meaning (sorry, Plato).

So if there is no God and no human nature apart from our free-will, how does the existentialist (always committed to a guide of living for the individual) determine what we should or should not do? Using Sartre's own example, we can see how the Sartrian distinguishes the moral from the immoral.

Example: Jean Pierre must decide to either stay home and help his mother or fight in the resistance with Sartre. He asks Sartre, "What is the right thing to do?" Sartre famously answers him, "Just choose my dear boy. By choosing you make it so." What does this mean? It means that there is no objective "right" or "wrong," but only what we choose.

However, Sartre is not a nihilist and does not want to allow anything to be moral so long as we endorse it. So what does he say? He asserts that, because the essence of humanity is the ability to choose, with every choice I make, I am essentially determining what an individual is and what we should be. Sartre asserts that when the individual chooses for himself, he ultimately chooses "for all mankind."

However, there is still no objective criterion such as God's laws or a kind of Kantian moral imperative within this theoretical framework to determine what is "right" and what is "wrong." But according to Sartre, one can choose badly. One often chooses badly when one acts out of "bad faith."

A "bad faith" choice is made when one looks purely at the facts to determine and explain what one should do. For instance, let's say that Jennifer is a Catholic but she really wants to get an abortion. However, she tells herself she would but it is a fact that she is a Catholic and therefore she is not allowed. According to Sartre, this line of reasoning is self-deceptive and is ultimately a mistake. If the universe is valueless then the facts of that universe are valueless as well. While it is a fact that she is a Catholic, she must accept full responsibility for whatever choice she makes.

The point here is not the morality of what she chooses (for Sartre makes no distinction) but the authenticity of her choice. Whatever she chooses to do, she must understand and accept responsibility for her freely "choosing" to give the tenets of the Catholic Church authority.

The fact that she is a Catholic and gives those teachings authority is wholly and completely determined by her free endorsement or "choice" to give those beliefs authority and meaning (i.e., she could obviously choose otherwise).

Sartre is important for illustrating a common kind of moral self-deception or laziness, where we say that "because I am X I cannot do Y and that's not my responsibility." But it is your responsibility, because you choose to be X in the first place and/or you choose to give that fact that you are X meaning and authority.

For Sartre, it doesn't matter if Jennifer is Catholic or not, or whether she gets an abortion or not. Sartre just wants to point out that we must recognize that we are wholly and completely responsible for what we accept and what we give authority and meaning to. We must recognize that we are responsible for our choices and our actions. The facts of the world and ourselves (e.g., I am a Catholic, American, German, Mormon or whatever) explain nothing in themselves, and only have the authority that we freely and authentically choose to bestow upon them. It really doesn't matter so much what we choose, so long as we choose it with sincere authenticity.

Sartre proposes one of the most radical moral philosophies in the history of the discipline, claiming there is no "right" or "wrong" but only what we choose. He is of incalcuable importance in twentieth-century philosophy and literature, and his emphasis on the absolute freedom and responsibility of the individual continues to inspire many thinkers of today. According to Sartre, we must be completely responsible for our moral choices and our moral lives. Well, looks like I just ran out of excuses.

*The more sand that has escaped from the hourglass of our life, the clearer we should see through it.*

*Man is condemned to be free; because once thrown into the world, he is responsible for everything he does.*

*Everything has been figured out except how to live.*

*In love, one and one are one.*

*Existence precedes and rules essence.*

*Hell is other people.*

*Slime is the agony of water.*

*What I like about my madness is that it has safeguarded me, from the very first, against the blandishments of "the élite"*

*When the rich wage war it's the poor who die.*

*A writer must refuse to allow himself to be transformed into an institution*

*The existentialist says at once that man is anguish.*

*There are two kinds of existentialists, those who are Christian and those who are atheistic.*

*Should I betray truth for the Proletariat or the Proletariat for the truth?*

*Three o'clock is always too late or too early for anything you want to do.*

*I have always been in agreement with the anarchists, who were the only ones to have imagined man complete, constituted by social action and whose principle characteristic was liberty.*

*Acting is happy agony.*

*Freedom is what you do with what's been done to you.*

*A lost battle is a battle one thinks one has lost.*

*Life has no meaning the moment you lose the illusion of being eternal.*

*Only the guy who isn't rowing has time to rock the boat.*

*Neither sex, without some fertilization of the complementary characters of the other, is capable of the highest reaches of human endeavor.*

CHAPTER TWENTY-THREE

# Ayn Rand

**(1905–1982)**

- Responsible for philosophy of "Objectivism"
- Influential supporter of capitalism
- Strong supporter of individualism

Ayn Rand was born Alissa Rosenbaum in St. Petersburg, Russia. Her father owned a chemist shop downstairs from their large and comfortable apartment. But even in her early childhood days, Rand longed to move to the West and become a great thinker and writer. In 1917, the first shots of the Russian revolution rang out, while Rand was daydreaming on her balcony. It would not be long before her father's store was nationalized by a communist gang, leaving the family in deep poverty. Soviet life just got

darker and darker for Rand, and the pictures of the West became brighter and brighter. In 1926, she left her family and her motherland, never to return. She arrived in New York City with just $50 in her purse.
For decades, Rand worked at whatever odd jobs she could find. But she did not give up her dream of becoming a writer and a great thinker. She was determined to succeed. In that she was much like the heroes of her books. That is to say, brave, individualistic, and steadfast.

With her 1943 novel, *The Fountainhead*, Rand revealed her philosophy of Objectivism, and went on to refine that philosophy in a number of works, both fiction and nonfiction. She died in 1982—a famous, wealthy, and respected philosopher.

## Rand's Big Idea: Objectivism

The holy trinity of Ayn Rand's philosophy of Objectivism is individualism, reason, and capitalism. According to Rand, the natural world exists. Its existence is not dependent upon our minds. She is a metaphysical realist in this way. Furthermore, she denies all supernaturalism, determinism, and fatalism.

The most important function of man, for Rand, is his capacity for *Reason*. Reason is man's fundamental gift, and with it he can uncover the laws and intricacies of nature. Reason is the process of conceptualizing; it is a tool used to understand and unify our world of experience.

Rand also supported what she called the "virtue of selfishness." This does not mean we can do whatever we want, but that the goal of human life is to attain happiness. To attain true happiness for the individual (the highest good for Rand), one must exercise Reason. Reason should guide our decisions and our actions. We gain self-esteem from acting in accordance with our Reason for the purpose of attaining happiness.

Rand's philosophy is similar to and perfectly compatible with capitalism, an economic system that she cherished. The implicit assumption of Objectivism is that by acting in accordance with our private interests, we'll also serve the interests of others. We should all act with Reason. We should act on behalf of our own happiness. We should act with self-esteem. If we all do this, says Rand, we wouldn't require a moral code based on meekness, selflessness, or absolute principles.

But is an action right if it furthers the happiness of the individual at another's expense? Rand claimed that an action that doesn't respect the rights of others is not a reasonable action (because most of us don't actually want to hurt others) and only reasonable actions lead to true happiness and self-esteem.

### Bessie Meets Ayn

If I decide to steal Bessie from Farmer Joe, Rand would say that the theft is wrong not because it probably wouldn't lead to my happiness.

Rand asserted that if every individual acted in a way to secure his own happiness, thinking primarily of himself, Reason would dictate a course of respect toward others' fundamental rights. But there are no abstract and absolute moral obligations to your fellow human being. Basically, don't give any unwarranted support to anyone out of a kind of Christian sense of obligation, and don't expect anyone to do the same for you. Act for yourself and use your capacity for Reason. If everyone did this, Rand contends, then individual lives would be more fully experienced and fulfilled.

Ayn Rand gave the optimistic values and assumptions of capitalism a philosophical coherence still admired today. God bless capitalism, God bless America, and God bless Ayn Rand. Oh, and I almost forgot, God bless Tiny Tim.

*The man who lets a leader prescribe his course is a wreck being towed to the scrap heap.*

*The ladder of success is best climbed by stepping on the rungs of opportunity.*

*Creation comes before distribution—or there will be nothing to distribute. Civilization is the progress toward a society of privacy. The savage's whole existence is public, ruled by the laws of his tribe. Civilization is the process of setting man free from men.*

*Upper classes are a nation's past; the middle class is its future.*

*Why do they always teach us that it's easy and evil to do what we want and that we need discipline to restrain ourselves? It's the hardest thing in the world—to do what we want. And it takes the greatest kind of courage. I mean, what we really want.*

*Throughout the centuries there were men who took first steps down new roads armed with nothing but their own Vision.*

*Man's unique reward, however, is that while animals survive by adjusting themselves to their background, man survives by adjusting his background to himself.*

*Every major horror of history was committed in the name of an altruistic motive. Has any act of selfishness ever equaled the carnage perpetrated by disciples of altruism?*

*Guilt is a rope that wears thin.*

*Happiness is that state of consciousness which proceeds from the achievement of one's values.*

*Thanksgiving is a typically American holiday. The lavish meal is a symbol of the fact that abundant consumption is the result and reward of production.*

*I need no warrant for being, and no word of sanction upon my being. I am the warrant and the sanction.*

*The evil of the world is made possible by nothing but the sanction you give it.*

*The Argument from Intimidation is a confession of intellectual impotence.*

*The spread of evil is the symptom of a vacuum. Whenever evil wins, it is only by default: by the moral failure of those who evade the fact that there can be no compromise on basic principles.*

*There is a level of cowardice lower than that of the conformist: the fashionable non-conformist.*

*The right to vote is a* **consequence***, not a primary cause, of a free social system—and its value depends on the constitutional structure implementing and strictly delimiting the voters' power; unlimited majority rule is an instance of the principle of tyranny.*

*Whatever their future, at the dawn of their lives, men seek a noble vision of man's nature and of life's potential.*

*I can accept anything, except what seems to be the easiest for most people: the half-way, the almost, the just-about, the in-between.*

*To love is to value. Only a rationally selfish man, a man of self-esteem, is capable of love—because he is the only man capable of holding firm, consistent, uncompromising, unbetrayed values. The man who does not value himself, cannot value anything or anyone.*

*My philosophy, in essence, is the concept of man as a heroic being, with his own happiness as the moral purpose of his life, with productive achievement as his noblest activity, and reason as his only absolute.*

*Men have been taught that it is a virtue to agree with others. But the creator is the man who disagrees. Men have been taught that it is a virtue to swim with the current. But the creator is the man who goes against the current. Men have been taught that it is a virtue to stand together. But the creator is the man who stands alone.*

*Integrity is the recognition of the fact that you cannot fake your consciousness, just as honesty is the recognition of the fact that you cannot fake existence.*

*Love is our response to our highest values. Love is self-enjoyment. The noblest love is born out of admiration of another's values.*

*Anyone who fights for the future, lives in it today.*

*Honor is self-esteem made visible in action.*

CHAPTER TWENTY-FOUR

# W.V.O. Quine

**(1908-2000)**

- Rejected centuries-old philosophical distinctions
- Immensely important twentieth-century philosopher
- Described language as a "web of belief"

Since the beginning of this book, we have seen two major strains of thought. One strain, the rationalists, believe that Reason is distinct from sensory experience and that it is the primary source of human knowledge. The other strain, the empiricists, claim that human knowledge arises out of our sensory experience, and say that Reason only serves to relate information that arises from sense perception. But both agree on one thing: Some judgments, like those of mathematics or logic, can be made without reference to any facts of experience. For example, Aristotle's law of non-contradiction states that P and not P cannot both be P. For what it is to be P, is to be P, and something cannot be P and also not be P at the same time. Virtually every philosopher we studied will agree that this is an analytic judgment. This means that the *truth* of the statement is logically contained in the proposition itself. Analytic judgments are separate from synthetic judgments, which require a synthesis of the facts of experience. Even Hobbes, Locke, and Hume would agree that the judgments of the facts of experience are separate from analytic judgments that contain their truth in their own logical construction. But the world of philosophy was shaken once again by Quine, who sought to blur the distinction of these two types of judgments.

Quine was born in Akron, Ohio. As early as high school, he showed a great aptitude for language and mathematics. A dedicated atheist early on, his quest for understanding the universe had to come from science and philosophy. Like many brilliant students of the time, he went to Harvard, where he became influenced by the work of Russell and Whitehead. After post-doctoral work in Europe, Quine returned to the United States in 1936. Over the next few years, he wrote philosophy, until he joined the Navy during Wold War II. In 1948, he became a full professor at Harvard. He died in 2000.

## Quine's Big Idea: Synthetic vs. Analytic Judgments

Just as part of Kant's fame is his distinction between these two types of judgments, Quine's fame consists in his blurring them.

Take the sentences:

1. All unmarried men are unmarried.
2. All bachelors are unmarried.
3. The bachelor is sitting on Bessie the Cow.

The third sentence is a synthetic sentence. Its truth depends on the facts of the world (i.e. that Bessie is really being sat on). The problem with the first two sentences, normally taken as being identical analytic judgments, is that they are not identical. The first sentence is a logical truth for Quine. Its truth is completely self-evident. It is just like saying all P are P. But the second sentence requires that we have a meaning and understanding of *what it is to be a bachelor*. We don't need to know what unmarried means to say that all unmarried men are unmarried.

So, what's the point? To have a conception of the word "bachelor" as being identical with the phrase "unmarried man" requires that "bachelor" be given a fixed universal meaning. To regard sentence two as analytic, according to Quine, requires a "web of belief" and a basic adherence to "metaphysical articles of faith." The consequence of this is that all science, history, geography, even mathematics, pure logic and physics, is a man-made web of meaning ultimately conditioned by our experience. Sentence two is only analytic if we understand the meaning of the word "bachelor." This meaning is only influenced by empirical experiences.

Quine believed we give words fixed universal meanings that ultimately create a "web of meaning" that only has value within the context of the culture. For example, once the word "earth" and the term "the center of the universe" were considered synonymous. Every scientific discipline, and the whole of human knowledge attaches to itself universal fixed meanings that are purely human creations. But experience can change these fixed meanings, such as it did in the case of the Copernican Revolution. What we take to be "true by definition" and therefore analytically true is actually revisable in light of future experiences. Everything is basically up for grabs. There is no statement or definition that is immune to further revision.

Furthermore, since the laws of logic are as distant from experience as possible, such as the law of non-contradiction (P and not P), even the laws of logic themselves are susceptible to *revision*. If this is true, then there can be no fundamental distinction between any analytic judgment and a synthetic one. Everything requires what Quine calls a cleavage or attachment to "metaphysical articles of faith."

Quine's investigation into the nature of language has had a significant effect on philosophy. Like Wittgenstein before him, Quine gave more evidence of the importance of language, and its impact on our interpretation of the world around us. Quine's work shows us that we need to accommodate the laws of logic to meet whatever new data science gives us. This can and should be done pragmatically, according to new evidence and information that comes to light. With Quine, even analytic judgments can be revised when new data is made available. Great, now we just don't know squat.

*Theory may be deliberate, as in a chapter on chemistry, or it may be second nature, as in the immemorial doctrine of ordinary enduring middle-sized physical objects.*

*The variables of quantification, 'something,' 'nothing,' 'everything,' range over our whole ontology, whatever it may be; and we are convicted of a particular ontological presupposition if, and only if, the alleged presuppositum has to be reckoned among the entities over which our variables range in order to render one of our affirmations true.*

*Scientific method is the way to truth, but it affords, even in principle, no unique definition of truth. Any so-called pragmatic definition of truth is doomed to failure equally.*

*Physics investigates the essential nature of the world, and biology describes a local bump. Psychology, human psychology, describes a bump on the bump.*

*English general and singular terms, identity, quantification, and the whole bag of ontological tricks may be correlated with elements of the native language in any of various mutually incompatible ways, each compatible with all possible linguistic data, and none preferable to another save as favored by a rationalization of the native language that is simple and natural to us.*

*The lore of our fathers is a fabric of sentences. In our hands it develops and changes, through more or less arbitrary and deliberate revisions and additions of our own, more or less directly occasioned by the continuing stimulation of our sense organs. It is a pale gray lore, black with fact and white with convention. But I have found no substantial reasons for concluding that there are any quite black threads in it, or any white ones.*

*What I enjoyed most was more the mathematical end than the philosophical, because of it being less a matter of opinion. Clarifying, not defending. Resting on proof.*

*To be is to be the value of a variable.*

*Different persons growing up in the same language are like different bushes trimmed and trained to take the shape of identical elephants. The anatomical details of twigs and branches will fulfill the elephantine form differently from bush to bush, but the overall outward results are alike.*

*Life is agid, life is fulgid. Life is what the least of us make most of us feel the least of us make the most of.*

*The strategy of semantic ascent is that it carries the discussion into a domain where both parties are better agreed on the objects (viz., words) and on the main terms connecting them. Words, or their inscriptions, unlike points, miles, classes and the rest, are tangible objects of the size so popular in the marketplace, where men of unlike conceptual schemes communicate at their best. The strategy is one of ascending to a common part of two fundamentally disparate conceptual schemes, the better to discuss the disparate foundations. No wonder it helps in philosophy.*

*I concur. . . in the opinion of the essayist that the status of expert testimony is the scandal and disgrace of the medical profession. The so-called expert is employed not because he is an expert physician, not because he is an expert diagnostician or an expert therapeutist, but because he is an expert swearer.*

*diagnostician or an expert therapeutist, but because he is an expert swearer. The philosopher's task differs from the others', then, in detail; but in no such drastic way as those suppose who imagine for the philosopher a vantage point outside the conceptual scheme that he takes in charge. There is no such cosmic exile. He cannot study and revise the fundamental conceptual scheme of science and common sense without having some conceptual scheme, whether the same or another no less in need of philosophical scrutiny, in which to work.*

*[It was] folly to seek a boundary between synthetic statements, which hold contingently on experience, and analytic statements, which hold come what may.*

*Any statement can be held true come what may, if we make drastic enough adjustments elsewhere in the system [of our beliefs]. The totality of our so-called knowledge or beliefs, from the most casual matters of geography and history to the profoundest laws of atomic physics or even of pure mathematics and logic, is a man-made fabric which impinges on experience only along the edges.*

*I do not do anything with computers, although one of my little results in mathematical logic has become a tool of the computer theory, the Quine*

*McCluskey principle. And corresponds to terminals in series, or to those in parallel, so that if you simplify mathematical logical steps, you have simplified your wiring. I arrived at it not from an interest in computers, but as a pedagogical device, a slick way of introducing that way of teaching mathematical logic.*

*Just as the introduction of the irrational numbers . . . is a convenient myth [which] simplifies the laws of arithmetic . . . so physical objects are postulated entities which round out and simplify our account of the flux of existence . . . the conceptional scheme of physical objects is [likewise] a convenient myth, simpler than the literal truth and yet containing that literal truth as a scattered part.*

*Our talk of external things, our very notion of things, is just a conceptual apparatus that helps us to foresee and control the triggering of our sensory receptors in the light of previous triggering of our sensory receptors. The triggering, first and last, is all we have to go on.*

*I am a physical object sitting in a physical world. Some of the forces of this physical world impinge on my surface. Light rays strike my retinas; molecules bombard my eardrums and fingertips. I strike back, emanating concentric air waves. These waves take the form of a torrent of discourse*

*I am a physical object sitting in a physical world. Some of the forces of this physical world impinge on my surface. Light rays strike my retinas; molecules bombard my eardrums and fingertips. I strike back, emanating concentric air waves. These waves take the form of a torrent of discourse about tables, people, molecules, light rays, retinas, air waves, prime numbers, infinite classes, joy and sorrow, good and evil.*

*Logic chases truth up the tree of grammar.*

*Life is a burgeoning, a quickening of the dim primordial urge in the murky wastes of time.*

*The desire to be right and the desire to have been right are two desires, and the sooner we separate them the better off we are. The desire to be right is the thirst for truth. On all counts, both practical and theoretical, there is nothing but good to be said for it. The desire to have been right, on the other hand, is the pride that goeth before a fall. It stands in the way of our seeing we were wrong, and thus blocks the progress of our knowledge.*

*No entity without identity.*

## About the Author

Like most aspiring philosopher kings, Gregory Bergman works for an investment banking firm on Wall Street in New York City. He studied philosophy at Hunter College.

## Acknowledgments

I'd like to gratefully thank the following persons: My father, who shows the courage of a lion every single day; Donna Raskin, whose comforting and informative correspondance I couldn't have done without; Brigid Carroll, whose clarity of purpose and good sense are second to none; Matt Marinovich, for skillful copyediting; Jennifer Beal for design; Professor Steven Ross, for his philosophical expertise and kindly advice; and Tara Hitlin, for while she did not contribute to this process in any way and was actually a hindrance to its completion, it is from her generosity that all good has sprung.

# ALSO FROM FAIR WINDS PRESS

**The Little Book of Bathroom Meditations**
Michelle Heller
ISBN: 1-59233-028-2
$9.95
Paperback; 208 pages
Available wherever books are sold

SPIRITUAL WISDOM FOR EVERY DAY

The book every bathroom needs to make it complete, *The Little Book of Bathroom Meditations* is a quirky, lighthearted collection of aphorisms, spiritual wisdom, and food for thought that can be read in a matter of minutes. Some topics covered include:

ACHIEVEMENT
**"If you find it in your heart to care for somebody else, you will have succeeded."**

—Maya Angelou

PATIENCE
**"There is more to life than increasing its speed."**

—Gandhi

Filled with quotes, parables, and wise words from such authors, visionaries, and figures from the past twenty centuries as Matthew Arnold, Kahlil Gibran, Jonathan Swift, Henry Miller, Charles Bukowski, James Joyce, Chaucer, Rabelais, and many, many more.